LOST RAILWAYS OF GLOUCESTERSHIRE

Stan Yorke

COUNTRYSIDE BOOKS
NEWBURY, BERKSHIRE

First published 2009
© Stan Yorke 2009
Reprinted 2015

All rights reserved. No reproduction
permitted without the prior permission
of the publisher:

COUNTRYSIDE BOOKS
3 Catherine Road
Newbury, Berkshire

To view our complete range of books,
please visit us at
www.countrysidebooks.co.uk

ISBN 978 1 84674 163 0

Cover picture of Kemble station
with ex-GWR 'Castle' no. 5042
Winchester Castle in 1959 is from
an original painting by Colin Doggett

Designed by Mon Mohan

Produced through The Letterworks Ltd., Reading
Typeset by KT Designs, St Helens
Printed by Book Press, Poland

CONTENTS

Notes on the maps   5

Abbreviations   5

Introduction   8

1 Northern Wanderings   10
  Ashchurch–Malvern
  Ashchurch–Evesham

2 Gloucester   18
  Two stations, two gauges, two companies and docks everywhere

3 Forest of Dean   30
  Lines around Cinderford
  Lines around Coleford
  The Dean Forest Railway

4 Gloucester's Western Links   53
  Gloucester–Ledbury: 'The Daffodil Line'
  Gloucester–Ross on Wye

5 Branches around the Forest's Edge   66
  Monmouth–Ross on Wye
  Monmouth–Chepstow

6 Cheltenham's Long Lost Links, Part 1   82
  Cheltenham–Stratford on Avon
  The Gloucestershire Warwickshire Railway
  Moreton to Shipston: the branch that time forgot

7 Cheltenham's Long Lost Links, Part 2   100
Cheltenham–Banbury
Cheltenham–Swindon (MSWJ)
Leckhampton Quarries

8 Southern Twigs   118
Kemble–Cirencester
Kemble–Tetbury
The Fairford branch

9 The Midland Railway's Branches   132
The Nailsworth branch
The Stroud branch
The Dursley branch
Sharpness and the Severn Bridge
The Thornbury branch

Conclusion   155

Opening and Final Closure Dates   156

Bibliography   157

Index   158

NOTES ON THE MAPS

I have tried to make the maps both clear and uncomplicated. Only two types of line are used – a dotted line to represent lines that have closed to passenger traffic and a solid line for those that still carry a public service. To aid the identification of stations, each chapter has its own map which, along with the overall map on pages 6–7, should enable readers to locate the various areas. All maps have north at the top. Restored lines are shown as closed but are given full coverage in the relevant chapter.

ABBREVIATIONS

The following abbreviations are used in this book:

B&GR	Birmingham & Gloucester Railway
BR	British Railways; British Rail after 1964
CMUPR	Coleford, Monmouth, Usk & Pontypool Railway
DFR	Dean Forest Railway
DMU	Diesel multiple unit
GWR	Great Western Railway
LMS	London, Midland & Scottish Railway
LNER	London & North Eastern Railway
LSWR	London & South Western Railway
MR	Midland Railway
MSWJ	Midland & South Western Junction Railway
OWWR	Oxford, Worcester & Wolverhampton Railway
S&WR	Severn & Wye Railway
SMA	Swindon, Marlborough & Andover Railway
SR	Southern Railway

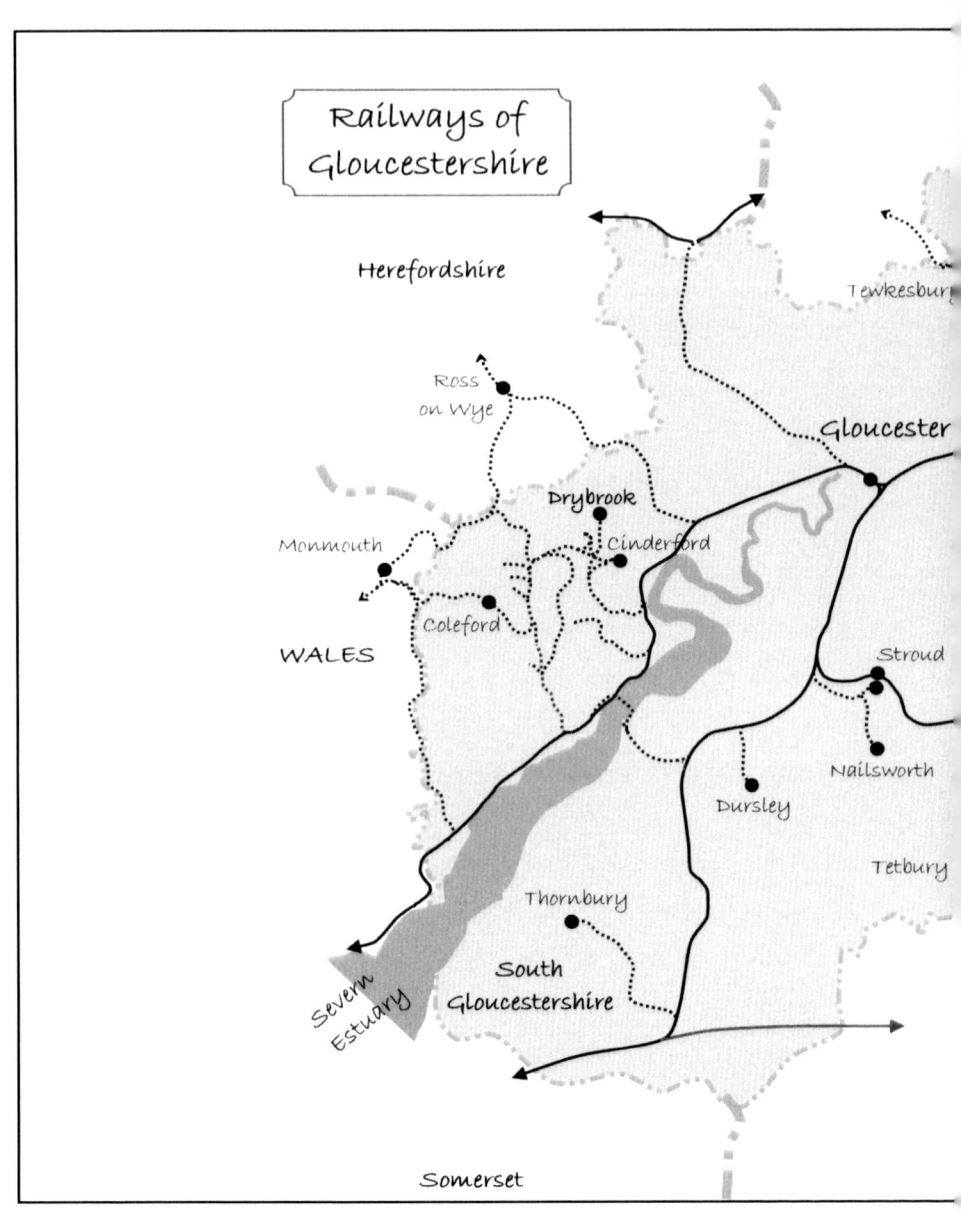

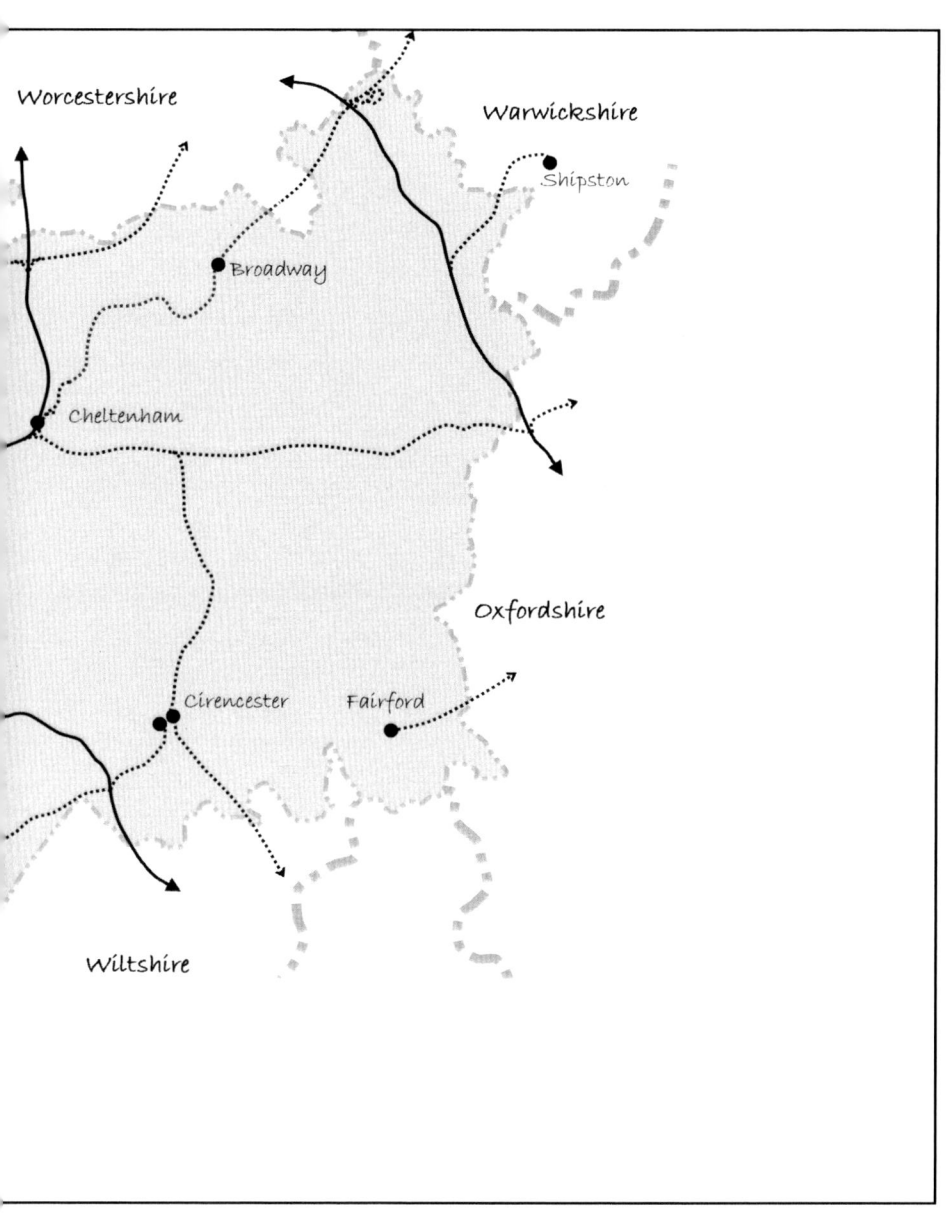

Introduction

Gloucestershire is geographically an unusual county, bordered by no fewer than eight other counties and itself divided by England's longest river, the Severn. Physically it is split into three great swathes running roughly north–south. To the east is the massive limestone plateau we know better as the Cotswolds, rising gently from Oxfordshire and ending in the dramatic escarpment known as The Edge. Within the Cotswolds we find dairy farming in the east, quarrying is extensive throughout and to the west was once the country's main sheep and wool industry.

Down the centre of the county lies a broad, fairly flat area of clay – the playground of the River Severn and home to the county's two largest towns, Gloucester and Cheltenham. Gloucester has been a port for centuries and became the natural route to the rest of the world for the industrial Midlands.

Across the river to the west is a quiet, hilly region – the Forest of Dean. Originally the second largest royal forest, it has been mined for coal and iron since Roman times. Its timber was used for ship-building and fed the country's biggest charcoal producing industry.

Each of these different activities needed transport in order to function, and early horse-drawn tramways featured in the Forest of Dean from the late 1700s with other tramways linking Cheltenham, Gloucester and Bristol.

Only two conventional canals plied their trade in Gloucestershire, the longest linking the Thames, near Lechlade, to the River Severn west of Stroud. Plagued with water shortages, its use collapsed once the railway route through Stroud was opened. The second canal linked Gloucester to Hereford but again lost out to the railways; indeed part of the line that replaced it was built over the old bed of the canal. The Gloucester & Sharpness Canal is a different beast altogether; it was built to bypass a dangerous section of the river and it carried very little local traffic of its own, though thankfully, unlike the others, it still carries pleasure craft to this day.

The long-distance main lines, normally the first railways to enter any area, arrived in the shape of the Birmingham & Gloucester, which opened in 1840, followed by the line to Swindon via Stroud and the Bristol to Gloucester line. These were joined in 1851 by the South Wales Railway between Gloucester, Chepstow and Newport. All these lines are still in use today and, indeed, with the addition of a line that runs across north-east Gloucestershire, these are the only lines that still carry passengers. Though promoted by independent companies, these lines soon became absorbed by either the Great Western Railway or the Midland Railway. A similar fate befell almost all the minor lines which found themselves totally dependent on the bigger companies. These were still private companies but, by the end of the Second World War, they were worn out and all but bankrupt. So, in 1947/8, the Government nationalised the railways to produce 'British Railways', a single countrywide organisation. Later, this title was shortened to 'British Rail' which lasted until privatisation took place in 1993/97.

But what of the other 250 miles of lines that were built with hope and enthusiasm but eventually lost the battle to the car and lorry? These are the subject of this book. We look at the history and services provided by these quiet rural byways. We must remember that when these lines were built people either walked, were pulled by a horse or just didn't travel. The railways were a revolution in terms of transport and, when we consider the list of towns served by these long-gone lines, we can see how vital they were to the development of the area.

In the book the lines are grouped into geographical areas with individual maps to help identify the closed stations. Photos of the stations when in use will, I hope, help the reader to imagine the days before the car, when the local railway was a vital link to the rest of the country. Where possible, I have also included photos of some of the stations as they are today, plus the two restored lines, which enable us to enjoy the smell and sound of steam engines hard at work once again.

Stan Yorke

1
Northern Wanderings

Ashchurch–Malvern
Ashchurch–Evesham

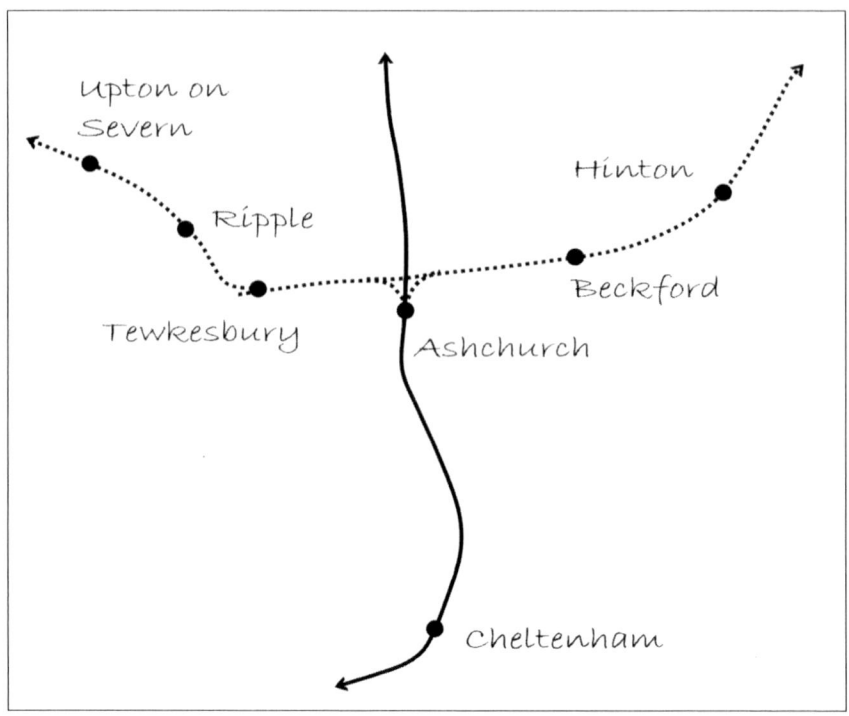

Ashchurch–Malvern

The main line between Birmingham (Bromsgrove) and Cheltenham had opened in 1840 and, in the same year, the company opened a horse-drawn tramway between its station at Ashchurch and Tewkesbury town station. In 1844 this service became conventional steam-engine hauled. The Birmingham & Gloucester Railway, including its branches, became part of the Midland Railway empire in 1845.

Ashchurch junction was very attractive, with pleasant buildings and the sort of layout one might see on a model railway – sharp radius curves serving the two branches. By the 1920s there were no fewer than three signal boxes, all of which were replaced by one larger box in 1958; but, with both branches long closed, this in turn closed in 1969, leaving the station controlled from Gloucester. Both main line platforms had ornate glass canopies held aloft by decorative cast-iron pillars. The two branches were linked by a double line, which crossed over the main line on the level to the north of the station, forming a large triangle. This link was reduced to a single track in 1927 and was

Ashchurch junction in 1949, with the Evesham line leaving to the right and the Malvern line to the left. The canopies over the main line platforms can be seen behind the signal box. The provender store is on the far left, as is the cattle dock. (Kidderminster Railway Museum)

Ashchurch today with a new, smaller station devoid of facilities but linked to a car park built over the old Tewkesbury platform and tracks. The siding leaving over the old Evesham line feeds a large Army storage facility. (Author)

lifted in 1957. There was a goods yard south of the road bridge, and sidings still remain in place today. A further goods complex was built north of the station, the main feature of which was a massive provender store, later used as an engineering works. Stopping trains on the main line ceased in 1971 but, following local protests, mainly from Tewkesbury, the station was rebuilt and reopened in 1997, with a large car park built over the old Tewkesbury platform and line.

Leaving Ashchurch to the west, the original branch line passed over virtually level ground for two miles and entered Tewkesbury, crossing over Cotteswold Road and The Oldbury to enter the station. The line then continued across the High Street, down Quay Street, where it served the Tewkesbury Brewery, and then over the River Avon to serve two mills and a loop on the quayside. Steam engines were not permitted to cross

Tewkesbury's second station, complete with newsagent's kiosk and decorative canopy. Taken looking towards Malvern, a couple of hundred yards behind the camera was the signal box at the junction between the new and old lines. (Kidderminster Railway Museum)

One of the few remains in Tewkesbury is the bridge over part of the Avon, now providing moorings for pleasure boats. (Author)

the High Street so these lines were worked by horse or tractor. This branch was in fact built to convey building materials from barges on the river to Ashchurch, to aid the construction of the main line.

In 1864 the Tewkesbury & Malvern Railway opened its line from a junction with the earlier line to the east of the town, where it built a new station, unfortunately in a far less convenient position than the first one. This new station started as a temporary structure, finally being replaced by a handsome Midland-style station eight years later. The old town station was closed, though the quay line was used for goods traffic until 1957 when the tracks were lifted. The signal box was built in the 'V' between the new lines and the old quay branch, as were the engine shed and goods facilities.

The new line was double track throughout and soon after leaving Tewkesbury station it passed through the 420-yard Tewkesbury tunnel and then crossed the Avon valley by a 62-yard bridge over the river, followed by a three-arch viaduct. The line now passed into the Severn valley, keeping the river some ½ mile distant for most of the time. Ripple station came next, serving a small village, and was provided with a single siding. Continuing north, the line crossed over the Severn and a mile later reached Upton on Severn station; alas, like Tewkesbury, it was on the edge of the town, which would help its demise in later years. As we are now firmly in Worcestershire I will end our journey here.

The service started with four through trains in the 1860s to which a further six Ashchurch to Tewkesbury local trains were added by 1890, which rose to ten by 1910. In the 1930s there were five through trains but only four extra local Tewkesbury trains. By British Railways times the service had dropped to just three through trains, plus another three locals to Tewkesbury. In 1952 the line beyond Upton was closed and the service was just one early morning and one evening train to Upton, plus four serving Tewkesbury. There was no Sunday service. Tewkesbury and Upton lost their passenger services in 1961, with the goods service to Upton ending in 1963 and to Tewkesbury in 1964.

Ripple station in 1958, with the down line removed, though it had not been used for passenger trains since the 1920s. Passenger services ended in 1961 and goods traffic just two years later. (Stations UK)

Upton on Severn station in 1912, looking back towards Tewkesbury. Passengers had to use the foot crossing between platforms. Upton was the terminus from 1952. (Lens of Sutton Association)

Ashchurch–Evesham

This line was the first part of a link that was to join the Midlands with the fruit and vegetable growing area in the Vale of Evesham. It also provided an alternative route from Gloucester and Cheltenham to Birmingham without having to climb the daunting slope of the Lickey Incline. It was formed from three separate companies but I will only look at the Ashchurch–Evesham section, which at least starts in Gloucestershire. This was built by the Midland Railway and opened in 1864, its double track serving stations at Beckford, Ashton, Hinton, Bengeworth and Evesham. Here there was a separate station alongside the GWR one (ex-Oxford, Worcester & Wolverhampton Railway) with extensive sidings, including a goods-only link to enable vans to be interchanged between the two companies. In later years this link was rebuilt to enable

Beckford station in the 1930s, showing the Midland Railway-style canopy over the platform. Note the somewhat flat countryside in the Vale of Evesham. (Lens of Sutton Association)

Hinton station in a delightful, early postcard shot from 1912. Two members of staff have joined four passengers and a dog for the posed photograph. Note the shunting in the goods sidings – probably coal. (Lens of Sutton Association)

passenger trains to run through and this route became an alternative to the Honeybourne–Cheltenham line.

The line was operated by the Midland Railway from the start and was always busy, at least by rural standards. The stations were substantial stone structures provided with goods yards to handle the extensive fruit and veg traffic. Though seasonal, this sometimes involved trains of up to 60 vans. Beckford village was under ½ mile from the station but both Ashton and Hinton involved a longer walk.

In 1962 British Railways announced the closure of the northern section to Redditch due to it being allegedly 'unsafe'. The southern section was closed the following year. In fairness the fruit and veg trade, of course, is spread over a very wide area and most of the traffic that came to the two intermediate stations was brought there by cart and, later, lorry. To go to the Ashchurch or Evesham stations instead would really make little difference with the improved roads of the 1950s. During the last war, sidings left the Evesham line, quite near to Ashchurch, serving a large Army transport depot and these still exist though they are rarely used.

2
Gloucester

*Two stations, two gauges, two companies
and docks everywhere*

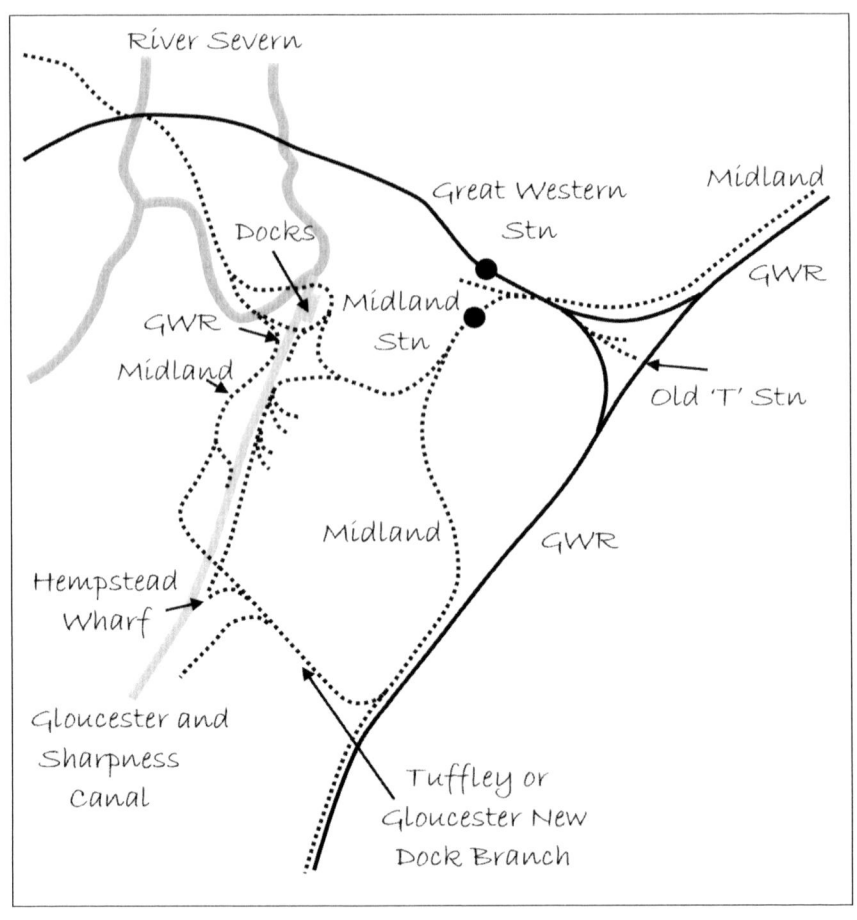

Gloucester's railways can at first seem rather bewildering, partly due to the competition between the two companies, the GWR and the Midland, and partly to the way in which the docks were so close to the town centre. Several sections of line had running rights for both the GWR and the Midland. Today almost all the city's railways have vanished, making the story slightly unreal.

Our account should start with the 3 ft 6 in tramways that reached Gloucester in 1810, but for simplicity I will pass directly on to the arrival of the first conventional railway in 1840. This was the standard gauge Birmingham & Gloucester Railway (B&GR), followed in 1844 by the arrival from the south of the broad gauge Bristol & Gloucester line. Thus was born the troublesome change of gauge that plagued Gloucester for the next 28 years.

In 1847 the GWR built its own station just to the north of the B&GR and added the so-called 'Cheltenham Link'. This was to enable trains from London (which arrived in Gloucester from the south) to carry on at speed northwards to Cheltenham without having to reverse in the Gloucester station. Some of these trains would stop at the 'T' station (named from its layout), where a coach or two would be uncoupled, shunted onto a turntable, turned through 90° and run onto the new line to go

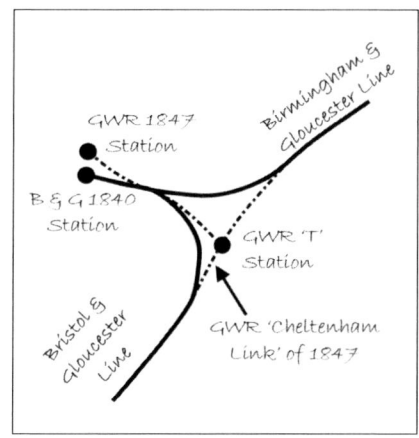
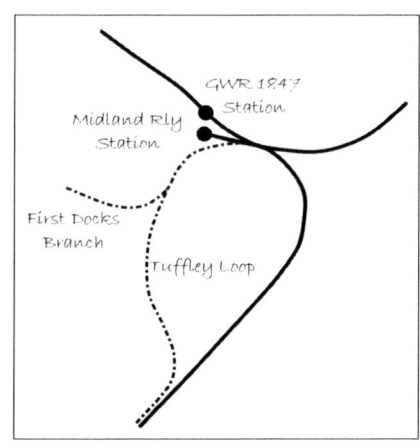

Around 1847   *and around 1870.*

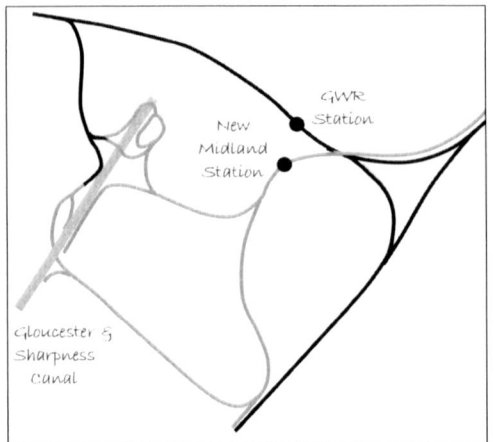 

The system at its peak around 1940   *and the system today.*

into Gloucester GWR station, a performance that only lasted for three years. In 1851 the South Wales line arrived, making an end-on link into the GWR station from the west. By 1872 all the lines were standard gauge but not before the GWR had laid its own tracks south to serve its Stroud and London trains.

Part of the dock area today, with some of the track in place and a few trucks to remind us of what it once looked like. There were several steam-driven mobile cranes, which would have handled the heavier loads between rail and the ships. (Author)

During this same period the Midland Railway had laid the Tuffley loop, which meant that its trains coming from the north could now carry on south without a change of direction. The dock lines were also laid in standard gauge, in many places simply over the top of the old tramway routes.

In 1872 the GWR removed the 'Cheltenham Link', having accepted that passengers wanted to be able to make connections at Gloucester between the three major directions. In 1896 the Midland opened a new station on the Tuffley loop (known later as Eastgate) so that its trains didn't have to shunt in and out of the old B&GR terminus, which then became carriage sidings.

In 1901 the 'Cheltenham Link' was reinstated, initially for goods traffic but by 1908 it was being used for fast passenger trains again.

The dock lines had developed to their full extent at this point and were probably at their zenith in terms of traffic. Note,

Gloucester Midland station around 1912, showing the wide platforms anticipating vast crowds. The train waiting to leave on the island platform will soon be passing onto the Tuffley loop on its journey south. (Lens of Sutton Association)

California Crossing in 1968 with the signal box seen in the distance in the shot below. (D. Stowell)

Down the Tuffley loop in 1975. Soon after leaving the new Midland station the line to the docks, known as the High Orchard branch, leaves the main line and turns right before the signal box. (D. Stowell)

This 1964 picture is taken from the north end of the island platform of Eastgate station and gives an idea of just how busy Gloucester's railway system was. (R. Carpenter)

however, how the Midland had kept the GWR out of the eastern (town) side of the canal.

The Midland station was built with three platforms on a long gentle curve. Two goods lines bypassed the station on the east side to keep the station free for passenger trains. The Tuffley loop had been laid at street level and involved five level crossings, a cause of great annoyance to the early motorists and cyclists of Gloucester. The GWR station originally had one very long platform, which by dint of central points could accommodate both eastward and westward trains. In 1914 the station was expanded with two long platforms but now there were four tracks and each pair had crossover point work near the centre, which meant that two trains could be brought into each platform if needed. In 1860 local industrialists had started the Gloucester Railway Carriage and Wagon Works, which for over 100 years produced rolling stock for railway companies around the world. The works were in the dock area and were linked to the Midland lines.

Both companies had large engine depots adjacent to their lines, plus large goods yards covering an enormous area between the two stations and the triangle formed by the main lines.

There were, however, still only two tracks north of Gloucester, which caused endless delays and, at the start of the Second World War, these were doubled to four tracks as far as Cheltenham.

After nationalisation in 1948 the boundaries changed, with the whole area coming under the GWR, and in 1951 the two stations were renamed Gloucester Central for the ex-GWR station and Gloucester Eastgate for the Midland. Both had always been connected by a 250-yard-long elevated footbridge, built as a compromise when the two companies failed to agree on a common station. It had no side windows, giving a slightly claustrophobic feel, and was not popular with passengers. The 1960s saw a steady drop in train services as more and more local

The GWR station in 1932, showing the two pairs of lines and the crossover point work that enables each platform to handle two trains. This station became Gloucester Central in 1951 and underwent major alterations in 1977. (Brunel University/Mowat Collection)

lines closed and lorries now served the docks, resulting in the gradual shrinking of these lines until the dock system was completely closed in 1971. In 1968 the four tracks going south were reduced to just two and in 1975 the Tuffley loop was causing intolerable delays at the level crossings and the decision was made to close it along with the ex-Midland Eastgate station. Further attempts to improve Gloucester Central came in 1977 when the long down platform was lengthened again. Now one of the longest platforms in the country at just over a third of a mile long, it became the only one used by passenger trains until 1984 when conventional two-platform use returned. The station is still inconvenient, with north–south trains having to reverse to continue their journey, a problem that led Virgin Trains in 2003 to threaten to stop calling at Gloucester altogether.

Today we are back almost where we were in 1845! Road building and retail development has rendered much of the vast old system invisible.

From the point of view of long-distance traffic Gloucester forms a crossroads. Good fast lines radiate north to the Midlands and beyond, to the east via the Stroud valley to London, to the south via Bristol and to the west by the South Wales line. When we add in the industry and customers that each direction generates the picture gets very busy indeed. From Wales came coal for London and the south, plus traffic from Ireland via Fishguard, which alone produced several mail trains a day. The north and east provided vast areas of population needing coal and food, whilst the south sent vast amounts of foodstuffs. Add all the local movement of agricultural produce and it is easy to see that Gloucester was a surprising place where, in the first half of the 20th century, an almost endless stream of freight trains could be seen night and day.

Through passenger traffic was equally busy. Trains had started to run to Bristol and in 1860 there were five each day. Six served Birmingham, and London had eight trains a day via Swindon. Connections at Gloucester enabled passengers to leave Swansea early in the morning and reach York and Newcastle that afternoon, which in the 1860s was quite revolutionary. By the 1880s trains from the Midlands were reaching Bournemouth

Shunting in the dock area not far from where the photos on page 20 were taken. This is a Midland Railway 1P class saddle tank. (Kidderminster Railway Museum)

An ex-Midland 0-4-0T 0F class engine no 1535 shunting in Bakers Quay alongside the canal opposite the Llanthony goods yards. (Kidderminster Railway Museum)

GLOUCESTER

(Above) Llanthony goods yard still busy in 1967. The canal runs left to right in the distance in front of the distinctive warehouses. (Kidderminster Railway Museum)

(Left) A similar shot taken in 1989 with the left and right hand sidings in the 1967 photo long gone. The lines were closed later the same year. (Author's Collection)

This is Tuffley junction where the Midland Railway from Eastgate station joins the original lines going south. Prior to 1968 both routes stayed independent, giving four tracks, but by December 1975, soon after this photo was taken, the Tuffley lines were closed. (Author's Collection)

and the south coast via the Somerset & Dorset lines, all via Gloucester, the best known being the 'Pines Express'. By the 1930s, trains between Gloucester and Bristol took just 43 minutes and Birmingham was reached in just over the hour. The famous 'Cheltenham Flyer' expresses used the bypass line and didn't stop at Gloucester for many years, the best completing their journey in 2½ hours. Through all this pounding speed the local trains had to fight their way, with stopping trains running south to Chalford, Nailsworth and Dursley and west to Chepstow, Cinderford in the Forest of Dean and Ross on Wye.

By the 1950s passenger traffic began to recover, in particular in the summer with through trains to Somerset, Devon and Cornwall, which packed the Gloucester lines on Saturdays. This short-lived surge probably made the dramatic drop in passengers in the 1960s seem even worse, as the car, lorry and coach stole the railway's traffic. It was, of course, inevitable; the new ways were quicker and more convenient.

By 1966 steam had vanished and the diesel reigned supreme as the railways struggled to find a new role. As can be imagined, with so much traffic coming and going beyond Gloucester's borders, all manner of locomotives could be seen. In the 1840s and 1850s, 2-2-2 locos were popular, plus 0-4-0, 0-4-2 and 4-2-0s and even the occasional 0-6-0. Many were broad gauge until 1872 when only standard gauge locos could work the area. Many 'singles' were still being used and turned in some surprising good work, particularly climbing up to Sapperton tunnel. Slowly, more powerful engines appeared, including GWR 'Aberdare' and 'Prairie' classes. Express duties fell to 'Saint' and 'Star' class engines. The hard-working 2-6-0 Moguls did sterling work on freight trains, though they could turn their hand to almost any duty if the need arose. By the 1920s the Midland lines saw the arrival of the famous compound 4-4-0s to the relief of some of the old Kirtley double framed 2-4-0 and 0-4-4 locomotives. By the 1930s GWR 'Halls' and LMS 'Patriots', 'Jubilees' and 'Black Fives' appeared, maintaining Gloucester as a fascinating place for train spotting.

An example of the movement of goods through Gloucester. A BR class 9F no 92250 hauls its train of coke wagons over the River Severn from Over junction and past the docks branch in 1965. (Kidderminster Railway Museum)

3
Forest of Dean

Lines around Cinderford
Lines around Coleford
The Dean Forest Railway

Lines around Cinderford

So much of the Forest of Dean's railway system was built to move the timber, coal and iron that passenger services between the centres of population came a very definite second best. In the early 1800s a large and sometimes changing network of tramways was built, often with alarming gradients, based around a line from Lydney to Lydbrook that had been authorised in 1809 as the Severn & Wye Railway and Canal Company.

Even before the broad gauge South Wales line was opened along the northern edge of the Severn river, a 3 ft 8 in tramway was built from Cinderford down to a dock at Bullo Pill in 1814. In 1823 it was joined by the Severn & Wye tramway, only to become part of the Forest of Dean railway in 1826. This in turn was taken over by the South Wales Railway in 1851.

The GWR rebuilt the line in broad gauge in 1854, thus linking Cinderford to the main system without a change of gauge. The line was extended northwards in stages until it reached Drybrook, though still only used for goods. It was from here that a single line carried on over the hills and down a long 1 in 30 gradient to meet the Grange Court to Ross line at Mitcheldean in 1880. This section never carried traffic and was left derelict and rotting, and by 1900 it was virtually gone.

In addition to the Cinderford line, the junction at Bullo Pill included a siding which gave access to the old tramway

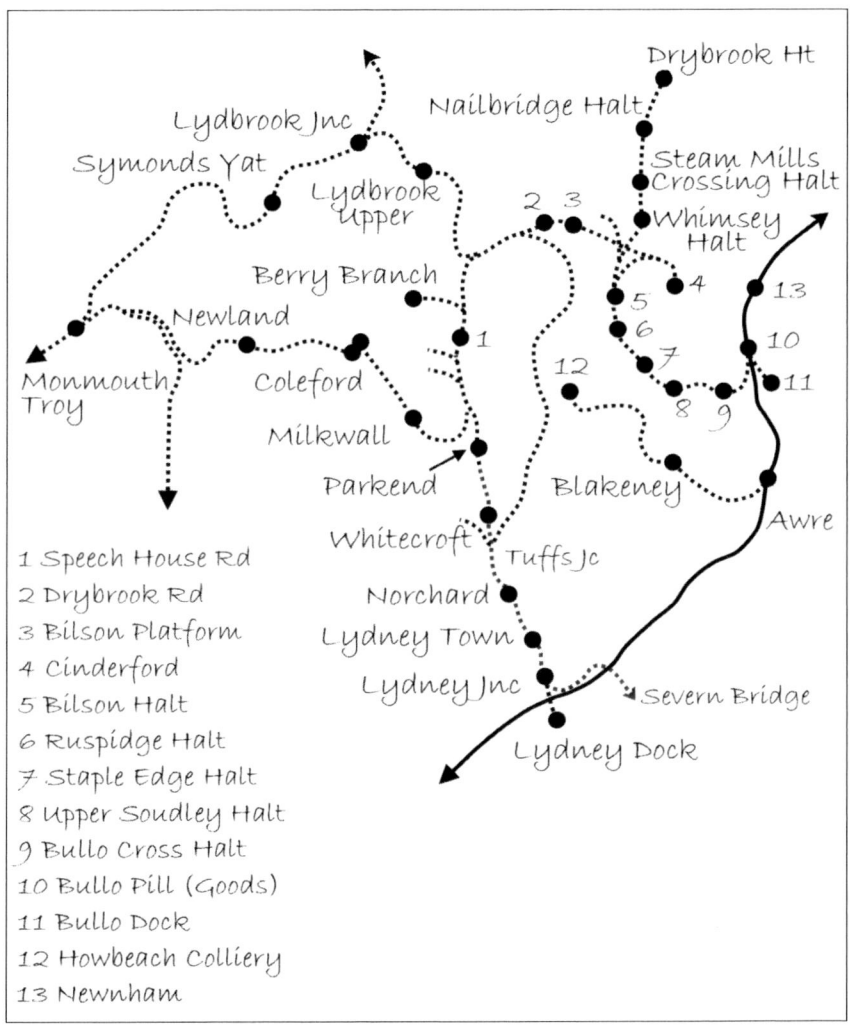

harbour. In 1926 the basin gates were removed and the basin became tidal, ending the coal loading here. Bullo always remained a goods-only junction and never had any platforms. When the GWR introduced a passenger service along this line to

Bullo Pill junction in 1946, with the Cinderford line climbing away to the left. The siding leaving the picture middle right went down to the old ex-tramway dock. (Kidderminster Railway Museum)

Cinderford in 1907, it operated from Newnham station to the north of Bullo.

Setting off from the junction, the single line turned west and soon reached the diminutive Bullo Cross Halt. Built in the standard GWR wooden style, it was close to the main road but very little else. A 1,064-yard-long tunnel followed, taking the line into Lower Soudley, where an iron works complete with blast furnaces operated until the late 1870s. Almost immediately a second shorter tunnel led north and into Upper Soudley Halt, which was opened in 1907. The line now turned northwards and passed through the Blue Rock tunnel into a valley lined with old coalmines, iron pits and limestone quarries. The next stop was Staple Edge Halt, which like all the halts had opened with the start of the passenger services. There was a siding that fed the Eastern United Colliery, which produced excellent steam coal until it closed in 1959. Still plying a northerly course, the next

Ruspidge Halt in the 1950s. Today the end of the siding on the right holds a Wiggins bitumen tank wagon, which would have been a common sight after 1967. (R. Blencowe)

The site today, providing a rest for walkers who use the area and adjacent car parks. (Author)

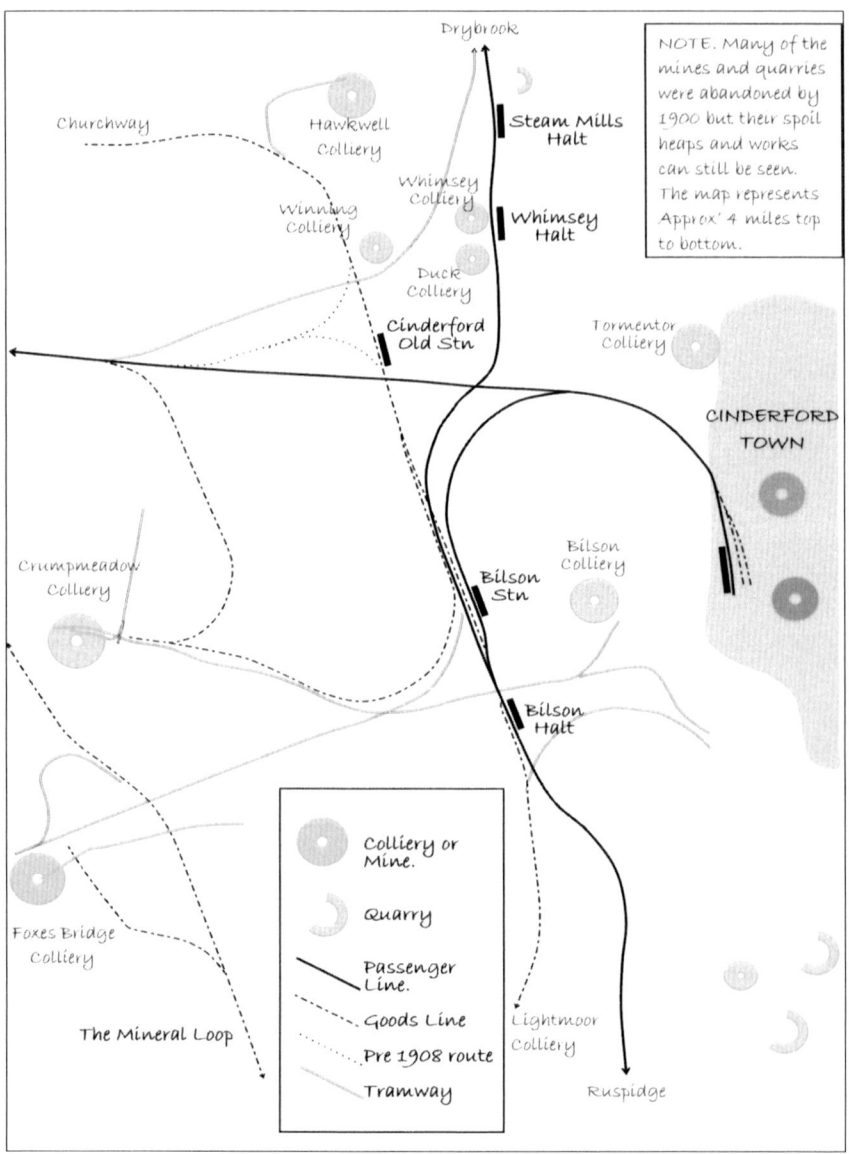

A sketch map of the Cinderford area, showing the numerous lines. Thankfully not all of them were active at the same time.

Bilson Halt in 1922, looking north. The siding on the left ran for nearly a mile to Lightmoor Colliery. (R. Carpenter)

Looking back towards Bilson Halt from the junction. Cinderford trains ran on the left-hand track before passing behind the camera, then sweeping round into Cinderford. (Kidderminster Railway Museum)

Cinderford station in 1912, with a train approaching, hauled by a class 2021 0-6-0 saddle tank. (Lens of Sutton Association)

Steam Mills Halt in 1952, which had a passenger service until 1930 but still saw occasional goods movement to Drybrook. (Brunel University/Mowat Collection)

station was Ruspidge Halt, with stone-built accommodation and a level crossing. There had been goods sidings here before the station was built, serving the inevitable collieries and quarries. From here the outskirts of Cinderford are barely another mile. For a while (1907–1920) there was a halt at Bilson where a mile-long siding served the Lightmoor Colliery, and a little further north came the old Cinderford station, used from 1878 to 1900. A second Bilson station opened just north of the halt, adding to the confusion in this area. Eventually, in 1900, a new Cinderford station opened for S&WR trains, built on the western edge of the town. The line from Bullo carried its first passenger trains to Steam Mills Crossing north of the town in 1907 but within a year a new spur was built into the Cinderford station, now served by both the GWR trains from Newnham and the ex-Severn & Wye trains from Parkend and Lydney. It had a single platform and a modest goods yard, with a goods shed, crane and cattle pens.

The passenger trains now continued to Drybrook, always calling at the Cinderford station and reversing back to Bilson

A typical steam rail motor of the early 1900s, though not in the Forest of Dean; this gives a good idea of what these unpopular carriages looked like. (Author's Collection)

before continuing north. The line to Drybrook passed through seemingly endless collieries and quarries but all set against a background of beautiful forest. Whimsey Halt opened around 1930 and handled goods traffic until 1967 when Barry Wiggins took it over to expand its hot bitumen business. Steam Mills Halt opened in 1907, followed by Nailbridge Halt. Tracing this journey today, our route follows earlier tramways whose earthworks can still confuse the observer. At last Drybrook is reached, with a single platform, opened yet again in 1907; this was at least in the village. The long disused line towards Mitcheldean starts with a short tunnel to which a trainload of explosives was dispatched for storage in 1940. Alas, nobody mentioned that the track beyond Drybrook had been lifted in the late 1800s! Determined to succeed, the next year a narrow gauge railway was opened into the tunnel so that the intended storage use could be achieved.

Passenger trains to Cinderford were rail motors or later single coach auto units with a 517 class 0-4-2 or a pannier tank. These set out from Newnham on the South Wales main line where a bay platform was constructed in 1907 though after the early 1950s the service ran from Gloucester, the bay being taken out in 1957. The passenger service from Gloucester lasted until 1958 and goods traffic until 1967, by which time diesels were used. Passenger trains to Drybrook had come to an end in 1930. The ex-Severn & Wye line into Cinderford was taken up in 1951.

The standard gauge Severn & Wye line, itself built along older tramway routes, changed to locomotive power in 1851, to broad gauge in 1869 and then back again just three years later when the South Wales line changed. It had an engine shed and repair works just north of Lydney Junction. In 1872 the Coleford branch was built (see next section) and the Sharpness to Lydney line opened (see Chapter 9), both soon providing better outlets for the coal, iron and timber. Alas, the output of the mines was now dropping off due to cheaper supplies elsewhere – the standard gauge railways had really arrived too late. The Severn & Wye, having been involved with the Sharpness line, was now facing serious financial problems and in 1894 it was vested jointly in the GWR and Midland.

The little Coleford branch from Parkend lost its passenger services in 1929, along with passenger traffic on the original 'main' section from Lydney to Lydbrook, including its line via Drybrook Road into Cinderford. These lines, however, continued to carry freight into the 1960s.

Passenger services were always fairly meagre; the Lydney–Lydbrook service peaked in 1910 with six trains, which dropped to just three in 1920. All called at Cinderford, reversing to continue. There were also three Lydney to Cinderford trains.

The original end of the line at Lydney had been the dock, a considerable stretch of water connected to the River Severn by a lock system. This had sidings on both sides, feeding manually operated coal chutes for loading into the small boats. These were originally tramways (until 1882) and were in use long before the South Wales main line came along; this crossed over the harbour line on the level and the crossing was rebuilt as each line changed gauge. The northern side of the harbour fell into disuse in 1927 whilst the southern side with its six coal chutes lasted

Lydney harbour line (up/down) crossing over the main line (left/right) in 1952. The roadway to the harbour follows our line behind the camera. (Brunel University/Mowat Collection)

Lydney Junction station in 1950, showing the 1908 elevated walkway back to the Lydney station on the South Wales main line. (Author's Collection)

Lydney Town station in 1947. The station was in the centre of the town on Hill Street, which crosses just behind the camera. (Stations UK)

until 1963. Once the harbour line closed in 1963, its crossing with the South Wales lines was removed within two months.

There were stations on both lines, the main line being simply Lydney whilst the Severn & Wye was named Lydney Junction. In 1908 the two were linked by a long footbridge and between 1955 and 1968 both stations were known simply as Lydney Junction.

The West of England Wagon Works fed into the line between Lydney Junction and Lydney Town and lasted until 1959. This had been a pigment works earlier, extracting colours from local iron ores. There was also a tin plate works, which had its own line to the harbour, passing under the main lines. Tin plate was rolled here until 1957. The Lydney area had other local industries and the town station was well placed in the centre. It had a small goods yard and north of the level crossing there were coal sidings.

Lydney Town station today on the restored Dean Forest Railway. It is somewhat shorter and on realigned track due to other developments. (Author)

Northwards the line became single track and at Norchard there was the Park Colliery, the deepest in the area but plagued with water, which needed constant pumping. This pit was still producing some 50,000 tons of coal per year in the 1930s, when a power station had been built next door and was fed coal directly by a long, covered conveyor. The coalmine closed in 1957 and the power station in 1967. This site became the base for the Dean Forest Railway in 1978, more of which later.

Next came Tuffs junction, where the Oakwood branch left to the west, feeding a chemical works, an iron mine and several collieries, finally closing in 1965. To the east the single track of the 'Mineral Loop' set off northwards to eventually rejoin the system at Drybrook Road. This line was built solely for coal, iron and timber and never carried passengers, eventually shrinking in length until the southern part closed in 1967. The line straight on entered the first station since Lydney at Whitecroft. The line from Tuffs junction was now double, including Whitecroft station, adjacent to which had been a factory making coal briquettes up to 1910, subsequently becoming a pin factory. Next came Parkend, again with two platforms and a goods yard. A branch to the west, the Marsh End sidings, was mainly used for loading timber and minerals. Just a short way north was the junction for the Coleford branch, which faced towards Cinderford, thus needing trains from Lydney to reverse to reach Coleford. This line set off, climbing at 1 in 30, a very severe gradient, which it maintained almost all the way to Coleford. The lines were six tracks wide at this junction but very soon all converged back into a single line.

The next station was Speech House Road, provided with just one platform. Here there were sidings into a local chemical works and an interchange with the Howerslade tramway, which lasted until the 1920s. Local goods traffic kept this section of the track in place after the section north was taken up in 1960. The line north reached a long siding to the Wimberry branch, which served the Cannop and Wimberry collieries, and continued then as the main line to Cinderford. Looking at the route today, a couple of miles before we reach Cinderford, the Lydbrook line, part of the original Severn & Wye line, comes in from the

A posed photo of Whitecroft station in 1912. There was a loop line that ran behind the left-hand platform. In later years only the right-hand track carried on, the left track becoming a long siding. (Lens of Sutton Association)

Parkend station in 1912, with the goods shed on the left behind the station building. The signal box was beyond the level crossing. (Lens of Sutton Association)

Speech House Road station in 1955, with a class 1600 pannier tank no 1625. (Kidderminster Railway Museum)

north-west at Serridge junction. This whole area is full of collieries and soon we reach Drybrook Road station where the so-called 'Mineral Loop' rejoins. This loop, which closed as a through route in 1942, served five important collieries. Originally the line turned south into Bilson junction but in 1907 was extended east and then south into a new station nearer to the town, later used by both the Severn & Wye line trains from Lydney and the GWR trains from Gloucester via Bullo and Newnham. The passenger service via the Bullo route proved more useful than the S&WR line and passenger services north of Lydney to both Cinderford and Lydbrook ceased in 1929.

Trains from Cinderford for Lydbrook turned right at Serridge junction and after a short section of level track faced a 3-mile descent at 1 in 50 interrupted by Lydbrook Upper and Lydbrook Lower stations before reaching Lydbrook Junction. Early along this section came three more collieries, which provided traffic into the 1960s, long after the passenger services ended. The Upper station had two platforms and a passing loop plus a small

Lydbrook Upper station in 1912, with a nice selection of wagons, including GWR, MR and those of a private owner. (Lens of Sutton Association)

goods yard, which stayed open until 1956. The signal box prior to 1929 was raised high above the station to give the signalman the ability to see more of the twisting line and its signals. The Lower station had only a single platform, which closed in 1903 though a long siding that dropped down at 1 in 25 to serve two tin works lasted until the 1930s.

(Left) The unusual elevated signal box in 1952, guarding weedy tracks into Lydbrook Upper station, 23 years after passenger services ended and barely four years before it all closed. (Brunel University/Mowat Collection)

Lydbrook Viaduct in 1964, unused for eight years and waiting to be taken down in the next year. It had a 5 mph speed limit. (R. Blencowe)

Lastly came a 187-yard long viaduct that took the line across the valley and after another mile the line curved into Lydbrook Junction and joined the Ross to Monmouth route.

Our last little line in the area was the broad gauge Forest of Dean Central Railway built in 1868. This was converted to standard gauge in 1872 and became part of the GWR in the 1923 grouping. It left the South Wales main line at Awre junction and served the goods-only Blakeney station and the Howbeach Colliery. Later it was extended through Howbeach Slade station to New Fancy junction where it reversed, crossed over the mineral loop and served the New Fancy Colliery. Traffic ceased in 1949 though the official closure wasn't announced until 1959.

Lines around Coleford

Our story starts with the horse and carts used to take coal, iron and timber from the Forest over turnpike roads to Monmouth.

This process was slow and relatively expensive. In 1810 a group of Monmouth businessmen obtained a Bill for the Monmouth Railway Company, which was to build a 3 ft 6 in gauge tramway from two mines and an iron producing furnace, the lines to meet near Broadwell. From here the line continued down a self-acting rope-hauled incline through Coleford and then by a twisting route going past Newland to reach the Wye valley near Redbrook, whence it descended through Wyesham and into a yard at Monmouth May Hill. There were incline connections to the upper and lower Redbrook tin works and a small wharf on the Wye.

In 1853 it was sold to the Coleford, Monmouth, Usk & Pontypool Railway who would have liked to convert the tramway to standard gauge. What the CMUPR did achieve was its line to Monmouth and, in 1861, it built the short extension over the Wye and into Wyesham, where it made a connection with the tramway.

In 1883 the GWR had purchased the tramway and rebuilt it as the standard gauge Coleford Railway. By now the 1861 extension was part of the Wye Valley Railway and constructing the junction in Wyesham posed no inter-company problems. Just two stations were built; Newland and the terminus at Coleford, which was next to the Severn & Wye Railway company's terminus. Both lines to Coleford had been authorised in 1872, with the S&WR line arriving in 1875.

Around ½ mile from Coleford the GWR line passed the extensive Whitecliff limestone quarry, which had originally supplied the iron smelting works in the area. Four tunnels were included to avoid the twists and turns of the old tramway but still the line had to contend with a fairly steep climb, Coleford being some 500 ft above Monmouth, giving an average gradient of 1 in 50. Both stations had passing loops, but the rest of the line was single track except for the section from Wyesham junction into Monmouth. There was a 20 mph speed limit over the line, which came down to 15 mph for any facing point work and down to 5 mph for Wyesham junction, where goods trains had to stop before proceeding. The passenger service consisted of four trains, two in the morning and two in the afternoon, taking

Newland station in 1947, remarkably intact considering that the track had been lifted in 1917. (Kidderminster Railway Museum)

Coleford GWR station and goods shed in 1950. The line from Newland entered top left but the three tracks bottom left simply fed a single headshunt. The just visible point, bottom left, was the original link between the two companies' tracks. (Kidderminster Railway Museum)

a gentle 20 minutes for the 5½ miles. Small GWR tank engines pulled the four-wheeled coaches, to which it was quite common to add goods vehicles. Alas, the very products it had been built to move were simply no longer economic to produce and the line was closed on 1st Jan 1917. Within two years the track had been lifted from Wyesham to the Whitecliff quarry, the line onwards to Coleford lasting until 1976 to move limestone via a link between the old GWR Coleford station and the Severn & Wye line that had been first provided in 1885. The original acts had allowed for a joint station but the GWR would have nothing to do with this; indeed the goods-only link between the two lines originally involved reversing four times, finally being relaid in 1951 for the limestone traffic.

The track at Wyesham junction itself was taken out in 1929. The tunnels at Redbrook and Newland stored ammunition during the Second World War and afterwards Newland tunnel was used to grow mushrooms – a rather sad end to a hard working little line that was simply built 50 years too late.

The Severn & Wye line left Coleford from its own station, a single platform affair with the minimum of passenger facilities, plus a small goods yard and shed. Despite many complaints the

The original Coleford Severn & Wye station in 1912. Both stations were well placed for the town though for some reason the townsfolk didn't seem to be interested. (Lens of Sutton Association)

Milkwall station in 1960, with the rebuilt brick building of 1923. The Sling branch enters through the grass on the left. The trackbed from here to Coleford can now be walked. (Lens of Sutton Association)

Coleford S&WR in 1923, with the newly-rebuilt brick buildings. At this time all the goods traffic had been transferred to the GWR shed though this meant lots of shunting. (Stations UK)

Today the old GWR shed houses the Coleford Railway Museum though it is difficult to place it in its original scene as it now stands alone in the middle of a car park! (Author)

building was not improved and in 1918 it was completely destroyed by fire. Between 1918 and 1924 various temporary structures appeared, eventually ending in a new brick-built station erected some way south of the original one.

The line set off towards Milkwall, climbing at 1 in 47; then, once over the summit, it descended at 1 in 31 to Milkwall station, passing three collieries and two brick works on the way. Here there was just a single platform with a passing loop and the inevitable siding, known as the Sling branch, which served several different coal and iron mines over the years. The little wooden station building was destroyed by fire in 1923, being replaced the next year, but alas the passenger service ended in 1929. The route from Coleford to Milkwall is now a public pathway. The line onwards to the junction north of Parkend had no stations and twisted and turned for just over 2 miles, clinging to the side of the hills above Ellwood until descending to the Severn & Wye main line.

The Dean Forest Railway

In 1974 a group of enthusiasts acquired the old Park Colliery and power station land and Norchard was created. Sidings were laid, along with workshops and a small terminus station and the

Norchard complex, with the restoration facilities spread out over the old Park Colliery. This was a drift mine and some of the shafts passed under the railway to the left. (Author)

DFR's rolling stock was moved here in 1978. The line between Parkend and Lydney had also been acquired and it wasn't long before steam trains were making runs between Norchard and Lydney. A high level platform was opened on the through line in 2004 to enable the service to operate over the recently reopened section to Parkend. It is quite impossible to describe the energy, determination and downright hard work that the volunteers put in over the intervening years; today it looks as though the line never closed, so natural and comfortable do the stations appear. The DFR still operates from Norchard, which has the only car parking – on the old power station land. Details on the website (www.deanforestrailway.co.uk).

Parkend station today, now the end of the line but once again served by steam trains. (Author)

4
Gloucester's Western Links

Gloucester–Ledbury: 'The Daffodil Line'
Gloucester–Ross on Wye

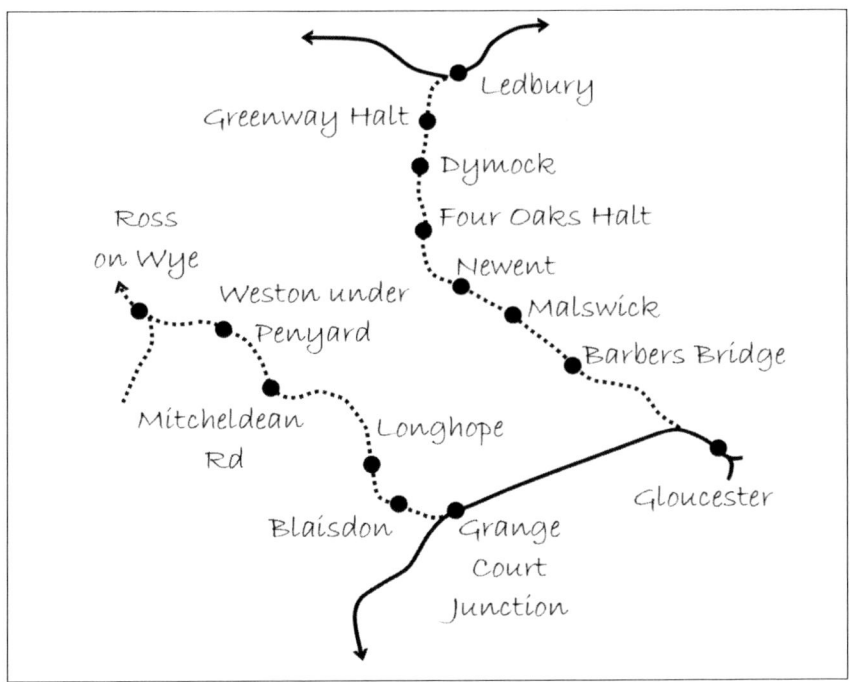

Gloucester–Ledbury: 'The Daffodil Line'

This delightful little line was born of two separate schemes proposed early in the 1870s, 'The Ross & Ledbury Railway' and the 'Newent Railway'. Both obtained their Acts in 1873 but alas, as so often, when the call went out for subscriptions nothing happened. No money – no railway, so in 1876 the two companies approached the GWR who agreed to raise the capital; but as part of the deal the old directors went and Sir Daniel Gooch (whose illustrious career in railway design and construction had begun in 1837 when Brunel appointed him his first Superintendent of Locomotive Engines) became chairman. This may seem a very generous move on the part of the GWR but they had in mind only part of the Ross & Ledbury route, which was to join the Newent Railway at Dymock, thus making a line from Gloucester to Ledbury. This afforded the GWR a much shorter route between Gloucester and the Midlands without having to go via Hereford.

Construction proceeded using much of the old Gloucester to Hereford canal, which was infilled and the trackbed built on top. The section from Ledbury to Dymock was constructed with double standard gauge track and though the earthworks south to Over junction were built to take double track, only a single line was laid from Dymock to Gloucester. There were three

Over junction, facing towards the South Wales lines and Gloucester. Looking every bit the important line it was supposed to be. (Brunel University/Clinker Collection)

The first station from Gloucester was Barbers Bridge, seen here in 1956. There had been a second track and platform but they had been unused since around 1918. (Kidderminster Railway Museum)

sections of significant gradient: each side of Four Oaks at 1 in 80 and the approach to Ledbury where a mile at 1 in 72 was followed by a mile at 1 in 64, which made it very difficult for goods trains. It all opened in July 1885 with very little ceremony and settled down to a typical branch line life. Both the original companies were absorbed into the GWR in 1892 though the line had been built with GWR money and run by them from the start.

The line was not a roaring success as a through route and when the GWR opened their North Warwickshire line in 1907, it took away any further ideas of the Ledbury line serving trains to the Midlands.

Early tender engines were limited to smaller sizes by the small turntable at Ledbury which they had to use for the return journey. The story goes that one Duke class loco was fitted with a small 2,000 gallon tender so it could be used on the line.

Economies started early in its life. In 1898 Barbers Bridge station, which was built as a passing place with two platforms,

Newent in 1959, when the line closed to passengers with everything still neat and tidy. (R. Carpenter)

Newent today buried in a maze of trees, though the platform can be traced. The station was quite a way from the town and this undoubtedly didn't help. (Author)

was reduced to a single line and just one working platform. By 1915 the northern end had been singled except for the junction at Ledbury, which had its own little signal box with just six levers, two of which were spares. This box was taken down in 1925, after which the points were controlled from the main Ledbury signal box.

A series of halts was added in an attempt to generate more passengers. All could only take one coach and had no facilities beyond a small shelter. They were Ledbury Town (1928), Greenway and Four Oaks (1937) and Malswick (1938). Dymock station was famous for its superb gardens and regularly won a 'best kept station garden' award.

Dymock handled a wide range of goods, including cattle feeds, apples and cider, timber (much of it for use as pit props) and, in late October, sugar beet destined for the works in Kidderminster. Newent handled similar goods, plus the usual wide range of rural products that we find hard to imagine in

Dymock station in its last year of passenger service, though goods work would survive another five years. Photographed in sunshine, it looks as though it would go on forever. (R. Carpenter)

Dymock today; all that is left is the bridge from which the previous picture was taken and faint traces of the platform edges. (Author)

these days of mass production. Both had a goods shed, cattle pens and coal facilities.

Each spring the area from Dymock to Newent became covered with wild daffodils, not just enough to make a pretty scene but vast quantities that were commercially cut and sent to London and the Midlands, thus giving the line its nickname.

The three or four trains each day were pulled by all manner of GWR engines, Dean Goods class, pannier tanks, class 4100 and 4500 tanks and 0-4-2 tanks with two-coach auto trains. Early diesel railcars appeared in the 1940s and stayed to the end. They were even known to have goods wagons added to make a rather odd mixed-traffic train. The junction into Ledbury was made single in 1957, with the Gloucester trains using the down platform.

The end, however, came when the line was losing money and there appeared no way to turn it around. Despite the usual inquiries and public meetings the line closed to passengers in 1959. The line from Ledbury to Dymock was lifted whilst goods traffic continued from Dymock to Gloucester until final closure

Ledbury station, with a train coming off the Gloucester branch in June 1959. (E.T. Gill)

in 1964. Just the day before, the line had a momentary flash of fame when three coaches of the Royal Train were drawn into the line near Barbers Bridge to enable Prince Philip to enjoy a quiet night's sleep before proceeding to Birmingham the next day.

Gloucester–Ross on Wye

This line was one of the early rural lines, having been proposed in 1844, but it only received its Act in 1851. The South Wales main line had opened in 1851 and our line was opened to Ross and Hereford in 1855. Though built with only a single broad gauge track it formed part of the GWR's first attempt to connect Gloucester to the Midlands via Hereford. An idea of its potential importance can be seen when, on the opening day, a special train ran from London, with Brunel among other GWR celebrities on board, collecting more dignitaries at Gloucester, before reaching Ross, where great celebrations took place.

Hardly surprisingly the GWR took over the line completely in 1862, and in 1866 the track was converted to dual gauge and in

Grange Court Junction station in 1923, looking along the Ross platforms, with the South Wales main line on the left. (Stations UK)

Looking in the same direction from the other side of the road bridge in 1932, we see the two lines veering apart. (Brunel University/Mowat Collection)

Looking from the bridge today, we just make out the path of the Ross branch to the right. (Author)

Though the local population is small and scattered, the station made a pub worthwhile. The sign is from the long closed station. (Author)

1869 it became just a standard gauge line, one of the first of the old broad gauge to do so. These early conversions were to make the route suitable for traffic destined for the Midlands. Ross became a junction in 1873 when the line from Monmouth arrived.

Grange Court Junction station on the main South Wales line became the junction for the Ross line in 1855. Situated in the space between the two routes was a large area used from 1901 by the Albion Carriage & Wagon Works. This closed in 1910 and the works were used by various other companies for some years.

At first there were two platforms but following the conversion to standard track the station was rebuilt with a full junction from the main lines and four much longer platforms, two on the main line and two for the Ross trains. A covered footbridge linked the two outer platforms with the central island platform. There were two signal boxes, built in 1897, which were replaced by a single box in 1935. A modest goods yard was provided plus long loops on both the up and down sides. Further sidings ran alongside both lines to the west of the road bridge. The station served the nearby village of Northwood Green plus a few well scattered farms.

Barely 1½ miles on our way, if tracing the route today, we find Blaisdon Halt where there had been a single siding from 1906 to serve the local village, which spread out around ½ mile to the north. As part of a general drive to get more passengers the GWR built a small single platform in 1929 and Blaisdon became a halt. Consisting of old sleepers filled in and surfaced, it had a small corrugated shelter. A simple path was provided from the road as it crossed over the line on a bridge.

Longhope station was well situated for its village, the largest on the journey to Ross. Two platforms and a passing loop were joined by a small goods loop, which seems to have been devoid of facilities beyond a cattle pen and a loading bay. The station building and a signal box stood on the down platform, facing Ross.

A further 3½ miles and the ½-mile-long Lea tunnel bring us to Mitcheldean Road, which served the small village of Lea about ½ mile away. Mitcheldean itself was 2½ miles away and very slightly nearer to Longhope! The station was a passing place

Blaisdon Halt in 1964, with signs of the long removed goods sidings on the right and time for a chat. (R. Blencowe)

Longhope station, with ex-GWR 'Manor' class no 7815 heading to Hereford via Ross on Wye in 1964. (Kidderminster Railway Museum)

with two platforms and a proper little goods yard complete with cattle pens and crane. Originally it had only a single short platform but these were doubled and extended in 1898. This was the end of the abortive extension line from Drybrook in the Dean Forest (see Chapter 3), the Mitcheldean end of which was used as a siding into the Wigpool Iron Mines until 1929. As at Grange Court, there was a pub just a few yards along the road, called the Junction Inn.

Again in the 1929 attempts to reach more passengers, another halt was opened at Weston under Penyard, which for a change was well placed to serve the village. This was a basic GWR braced timber platform with a simple shelter but no other facilities.

We had entered Herefordshire just before Lea tunnel but to make sense of the route I am including the line as far as Ross in this book.

Ross station, despite being fed by three single-track lines, was itself quite grand. It had two through platforms and a bay normally used by the Monmouth train. This bay was unusual in that it had a run round loop though it was rarely needed. There was a substantial goods shed and yard with all the usual

Mitcheldean Road station in 1959, looking spick and span as so many of these rural stations did right up to the end. (Kidderminster Railway Museum)

Ross on Wye station in 1923, with a Gloucester train arriving from Hereford. (Stations UK)

facilities. A small turntable (until 1939) and an engine shed were situated in the 'V' between the Gloucester and Monmouth lines. A glassed-in footbridge linked the two platforms.

Pre-war class 2301 and class 2251 0-6-0 tender locomotives worked the line plus class 43xx Moguls joined by 2-6-2 tanks and class 4300 engines. Even the occasional 'Hall' class passed through.

The passenger service was fairly constant at the five to seven trains a day level, originally starting at Grange Court but fairly early on running to and from Gloucester. As so often happened, there was a slight increase in the 1950s to eight trains but the end came very soon after in 1964 as part of Dr Beeching's axe. There had been a single Sunday train up to the 1930s. The journey time from Grange Court to Ross was around half an hour. Occasionally the line saw main line trains pass through when the Severn tunnel was closed for maintenance.

Today the section within Gloucester has completely disappeared, and even Ross station has been brushed away for modern commercial development. Its station building, however, does live on in a replica built for the terminus of the Severn Valley Railway in Kidderminster.

5
Branches around the Forest's Edge

Monmouth–Ross on Wye
Monmouth–Chepstow

Monmouth–Ross on Wye

The idea of a rail link between Monmouth and Ross on Wye was first mooted in the 1830s but the railway world was still occupied with plotting out the main lines and a rural branch had little hope. In 1855 the GWR opened the Hereford, Ross & Gloucester Railway, a broad gauge line, which gave Ross its station and the idea of how useful it is to be linked to two important cities.

Our line was born in 1864 when the Ross & Monmouth Railway Company was formed and over the following two years planning and the issue of shares took place. There were hopes not only of traffic between the two towns but also of goods traffic from a cable works at English Bicknor near Lydbrook, plus several quarries and the inevitable agricultural traffic. Worries over land ownership and the neighbouring Severn & Wye Railway were resolved with agreement to make Lydbrook the junction between the two lines. Building started at the Ross end and work started on Coppet Hill tunnel. Fortunately, in 1867, the Hereford, Ross & Gloucester line was converted to standard gauge, thus removing the change of gauge problems that were becoming a serious issue for the GWR. Work continued slowly, hindered by the usual cash problems, which had been exacerbated by the contractor insisting on being paid in cash and not in shares as was quite often done. In 1871 the

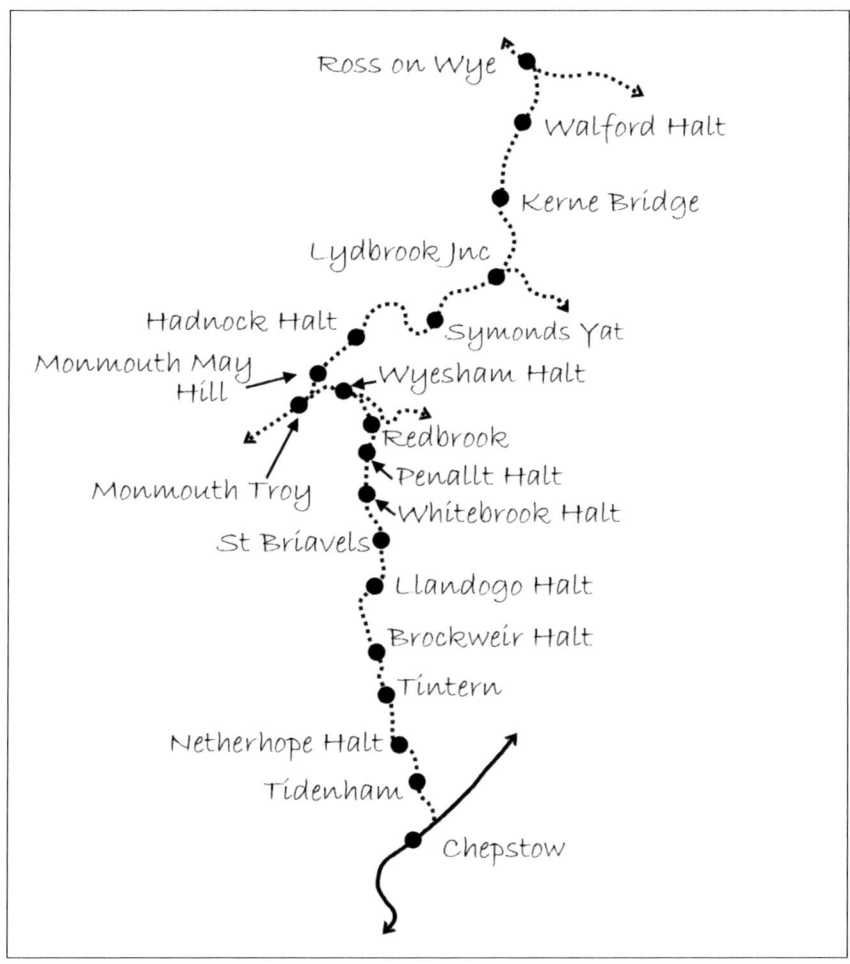

GWR entered the scene by negotiating new contracts with the builders and setting up arrangements for the GWR to operate the line when completed.

Delays still occurred, particularly over the supply of iron, but in 1873 the line finally opened – but only after a last minute panic when it was realised that Monmouth station did not have

Ross on Wye station in 1961. Although the Monmouth trains had ceased, their line is still clear, branching to the right. The Gloucester trains still had another three years to run. (Kidderminster Railway Museum)

A similar shot of Ross on Wye a couple of years later, showing the long disused engine shed. (R. Blencowe)

Today the engine shed is all that's left, now used by a garden centre. Everything else has disappeared under redevelopment. (Author)

a turntable. This was resolved by agreeing to use just tank engines rather than tender locomotives. The Monmouth end was at the temporary May Hill station, erected whilst the river bridge was being completed after which Monmouth Troy became the main station. May Hill was still found to be useful and was rebuilt as a permanent station, though neither station was that well placed for the town.

The line was fairly easy with just two gradients of 1 in 100 near to Ross. Kerne Bridge had two platforms and a passing loop along with sidings but the loop was taken out of use as early as 1901. Lydbrook Junction was by far the largest station with four platforms, two for the Monmouth–Ross line and two for the Severn & Wye line; four sidings were provided plus a siding into the cable works (Edison Swan from 1926 and AEI from 1961) though the point work was changed several times over its life. The sidings were all taken out by 1949 except for the cable works, which lasted until 1965. Symonds Yat was the tourist

One of two extra halts, this is Walford in 1965 after all services had ended, though the rails still look used. (Kidderminster Railway Museum)

Kerne Bridge in 1961, in its single-track goods-only days. (Stations UK)

Lydbrook Junction, shown here in 1923. The platforms for the S&WR line to Cinderford are on the far right. (Stations UK)

Symonds Yat was the busiest station for tourists though, as can be seen, only one platform was in use in this 1957 photograph. (Kidderminster Railway Museum)

This is Monmouth May Hill in 1923; the river stands between it and the town, though the main road bridge is just out of shot to the left. (Stations UK)

The bridge across the river needed to reach Monmouth Troy station. Today it is a footpath. (Author)

honey-pot, built with two platforms and a passing loop, which survived until 1953. A large hotel was erected by the station, along with the usual tearooms to refresh those who had climbed the local hills.

At the end of the first five years, the line had carried nearly 200,000 passengers but the goods traffic at 38,000 tons was viewed as disappointing. Nevertheless, the line made a profit right through to the 1923 grouping and was always tidy and neat. The only drama was the occasional flooding of the line near Kerne Bridge when the river was swollen by heavy rain.

Following the grouping little changed – this had after all always been GWR territory. The usual arrangement was to have just one engine in steam, usually a 0-4-2 or 0-6-2 tank, which trundled two coaches up and down the line six times each day and twice on Sundays. The train was rather unkindly nicknamed the 'Monmouth Bullet' though the 30-minute journey time was typical for such a rural line. An extra service between Ross and Lydbrook was also provided. Two further halts were opened, Walford in 1931 and Hadnock in 1951.

Better roads between Ross and Monmouth and the inevitable rise of buses, cars and the lorry meant that traffic gently faded in

Monmouth Troy station in 1923, looking back towards Ross. Though now over the river, the town was still a fair way off. (Stations UK)

the 1940s and 50s. The lack of any sizeable village on the route didn't help and in 1959 the last passenger train ran. Goods traffic continued, though the section from Lydbrook to Monmouth was soon shut, but even the Ross to Lydbrook freight ended in 1965.

Monmouth–Chepstow

The valley of the River Wye had an extensive history before the age of the railway. Tintern Abbey had been built in 1131, and the local mineral wealth was long known of, the first manufacture of brass in Britain having taken place in 1568 at Tintern. Flat-bottomed trows plied the river, carrying timber, coal and limestone for building, bound for Bristol and Gloucester. The beauty of the valley was already well appreciated with the birth of tourism in the late 1700s. In 1826 a turnpike road was opened along the valley and soon coaches and charabanc tours invaded the area.

In a pleasant change from many rural lines, the promoters of the railway along the valley had two quite clear objectives in mind – the first being the joining of Chepstow and Monmouth and the fact that such a link would offer an alternative route from Bristol, northwards through Ross on Wye and Hereford and thence to the Midlands. The second was straightforward tourism. Both seemed well proven reasons when the first proposals for a railway appeared in 1865 with the Wye Valley Railway Bill being submitted to Parliament in 1866 and passed. Unfortunately this was the year when the railway mania bubble burst and the country experienced one of the worst financial crashes of the century. During the following eight years the board of directors changed completely, with all members now being businessmen of considerable experience but none having any local connection. In 1874 construction began and after 2½ years' work the contractors, Messrs Reed Bros of London, completed the 13½ miles from the South Wales line east of Chepstow to Wyesham where a line into Monmouth already existed (see Chapter 3). It opened to the public in November 1876 with an agreement for the GWR to work the line and to lease it in perpetuity for a payment of around 50% of the gross receipts. The southern part of the line below Tintern contained all the difficult construction work, including two tunnels, one of which, Tidenham, was 1,188 yards long, took over 1½ years to construct and consumed much of the capital. There were four river crossings plus one on the Abbey works branch (see below). Fortunately, two of these, at Chepstow and Monmouth, had already been built by others.

Alas though, the company made almost no money. The usual reasons of bad weather affecting the tourist trade and the slow loss of small businesses, which was common throughout the turn of the century, did little to cheer the shareholders. In the original building a branch was constructed across the river just south of Tintern tunnel to serve the village and it was extended into the Abbey Wire & Tinplate Company's works. Though this had cost the company money it received no fees from the branch. The works closed in 1902 but the branch saw horse-drawn traffic to a small sawmill until 1935, with the track being lifted in 1941. Continuous squabbles with the GWR resulted in a low morale and poor services, which did little to encourage passengers. Irregularities led to action being taken against the chairman and other board members and in 1881 the shareholders appointed a

The viaduct that carried the railway across the low land beside the River Wye which was crossed by a long gone bridge just to the left. (Author)

Redbrook station in 1922, looking towards the bridge that would take the line to the west bank of the Wye. Tinplate was produced near here until 1961. (Kidderminster Railway Museum)

receiver. A new chairman and board were put in place but the poor running deterred the tourists and the long-distance traffic never came, and so in 1889 a receiver was again appointed. Eventually, in 1904, the line was sold to the GWR at a terrible loss to the shareholders. In a familiar pattern, the GWR had crippled a small line, which it then purchased for a bargain price and promptly brought it up to scratch.

I will take a quick look at the original stations as we journey down this most attractive of routes. After leaving Monmouth the line keeps to the eastern side of the river until Redbrook on Wye, which had one platform with a single storey station building plus a small signal box. A single goods loop was provided, with a shed and crane, which survived until 1964. Tinplate had been manufactured in Redbrook since the days of the tramways and lasted into the 1960s. The line now swings across the river on a 100-yard bridge held on four pairs of iron pillars, bolted onto which was a footpath, still in use today.

The single track of the Redbrook Viaduct and, on the left, the footpath still in use today. (Author)

The viaduct from the east river bank. The public house that can just be seen under the leftmost span received its beer by train. (Author)

Next is St Briavels, originally named Bigsweir, then until 1927 it became St Briavels & Llandogo. The village is a hard 2-mile climb from the station but despite its lonely position it performed a useful service. In the 1920s over 9,000 tickets were sold, and nearly 6,000 parcels and over 5,000 tons of goods were carried each year. The station was the usual small, stone building with a signal box and level crossing over what today is the A466. It is strange to realise that the train crew opened the gates themselves right into the 1960s. A goods loop and siding served a goods shed with the usual yard crane, worked until 1959 when freight traffic ended. There was an interesting combined weighbridge, which could take a single rail wagon or a small road vehicle.

Tintern was the next full station and was the most important of the stops. It was provided with the only passing loop on the line and three platform faces, plus a three siding goods yard with shed and crane. The station building was reached by a short drive from the main road, though it wasn't well sited for the village or the abbey. Today the station and signal box are used as a tourist centre. The next stretch of the line was the most costly to

St Briavels in 1932. It was surprisingly busy for such a modest and lonely station. The signal box is just in view on the near left. (Brunel University/Mowat Collection)

Tintern in 1955, showing the three platforms and signal box, looking towards Chepstow. The auto train is heading back to Monmouth. (Kidderminster Railway Museum)

The scene today, less the canopy and seats on the island platform and busy with tourists. (Author)

The Wireworks bridge, which was used until 1902, and then again with horses pulling the wagons serving a saw mill until 1935. Today it carries a footpath. (D. Stowell)

Netherhope Halt and the end of the costly tunnel, photographed in 1958. Access was by a footpath just behind the corrugated shelter. (Stations UK)

Tidenham station in better times in 1949, still with a staff and some goods traffic. (Kidderminster Railway Museum)

construct. On leaving Tintern the line crosses the river again, on a 69-yard bridge, and then plunges into the 182-yard Tintern tunnel to reappear above the river once more. At this point the little Abbey works siding left the line, clinging to the edge of the river valley before crossing over on its own bridge. Nearly 2 miles on, we come to the quarry opened in 1931 by Tintern Quarries Ltd, though it changed ownership during its 55 years. Next is Tidenham tunnel followed by Tidenham station, which had a single platform, a goods loop and a small shed. Behind the station was the Dayhouse Quarry, which was served by its own loop but, in 1968, this was relaid to handle the heavy traffic that lasted until 1990, long after all other traffic on the line had ended.

A service of four or five trains each way ran through to the late 1930s, joined by summer tourist trains. During this same period the GWR built six new halts to try and improve local patronage, at Whitebrook (1927), Llandogo (1927), Brockweir (1927), Wyesham (1931), Penallt (1931) and Netherhope (1932). Originally only Tintern had a passing loop though others were added and the busy summer service kept the signalmen on their toes. The journey now took some 50 minutes with 12 stops. Despite all this good effort the line was still losing money and even with the introduction of steam railcars and then diesel railcars it was obvious that it could not go on. Passenger traffic thus ceased in 1959, to be followed by goods services in 1964.

6
Cheltenham's Long Lost Links, Part 1

Cheltenham–Stratford on Avon
The Gloucestershire Warwickshire Railway
Moreton to Shipston: the branch that time forgot

Cheltenham–Stratford on Avon

Cheltenham is unusual in that it sprouted three long-distance branches, all of which formed part of long-distance cross-country links – a recipe that one might have thought would have brought fortune to both the area and the railways. Alas, in the 1800s when these lines were planned, local rivalry and getting a foothold into a neighbouring company's empire counted for far more than whether or not a route was viable.

The line started in 1859 as a branch from the Oxford to Worcester line at Honeybourne to Stratford on Avon, opened by the Oxford, Worcester & Wolverhampton Railway. Many years were to pass before the next section opened under the GWR in 1902 when the new line set out south-west from Honeybourne, reaching Toddington in 1904. Winchcombe was reached a year later and finally, in 1906, the line got to Cheltenham. It had been built to rival the nearby Midland Railway route from the Gloucester area via Cheltenham towards Birmingham and was built with double track, easy gradients and wide curves, in expectation of much through traffic. The original section to Stratford was doubled in 1907 to complete the through route.

As befits a line built for heavy through traffic, the construction involved several long embankments and viaducts. The goods area at Broadway station was built on made up ground, and to

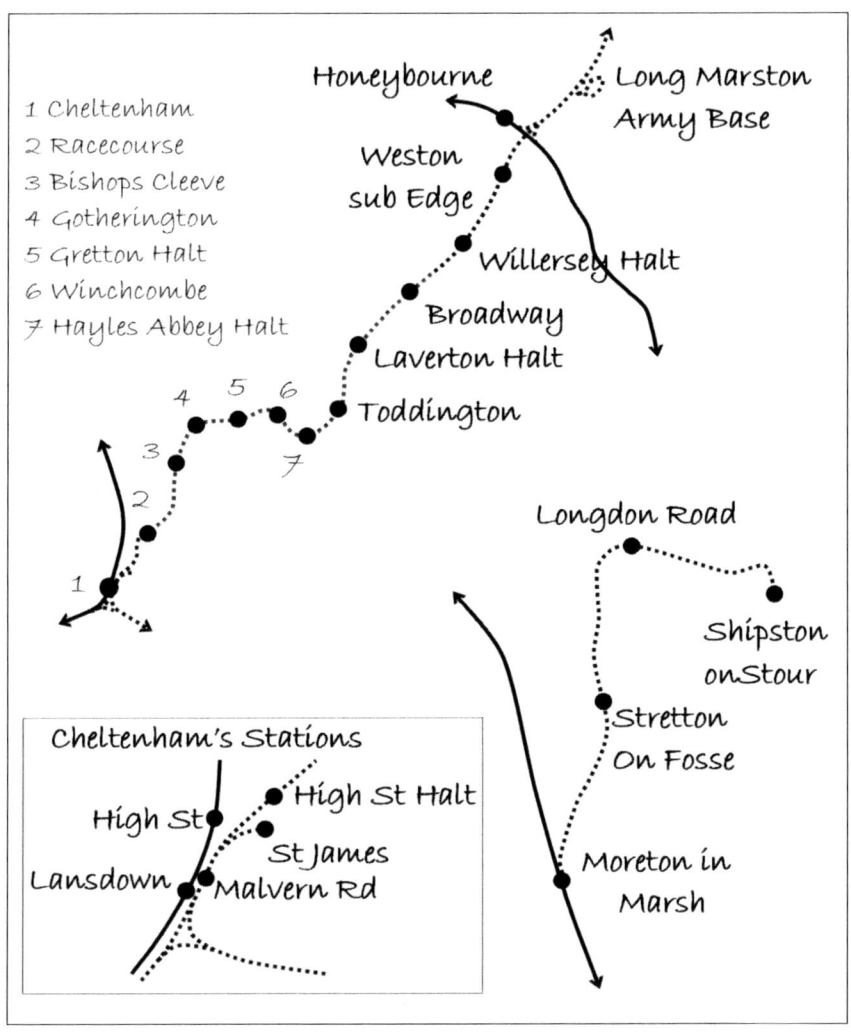

prevent the goods shed from subsiding it was placed on concrete pillars that went down onto the original ground level. South of Laverton is the Stanway Viaduct of 15 arches, each of 36 ft span and 46 ft high, built in blue Staffordshire brick. During construction, after 10 arches were complete, workers were

Honeybourne Junction station in 1962. Most of the local trains from Cheltenham terminated here. The start of the complex junction can just be seen through the bridge. (R. Blencowe)

removing the timber framing (formwork) used to hold up the arches whilst the cement became hard and the brickwork became strong. There was a steam crane above arch number 10 when the arch collapsed, killing two men instantly. The crane driver survived the fall and was taking shelter under arch number 9 when that collapsed. He was rescued but 40 minutes later was further injured when arch 8 collapsed. He died that night along with another injured workman; the date was Friday, the 13th. No single cause was found but the formwork was left in place much longer when the arches were rebuilt.

I will start our journey south of Stratford on Avon at the first station, Milcote, which had the old Gloucestershire county border passing through its southern end, though the line pops in and out of Gloucestershire several times. As built in 1859 it had a single platform south of the level crossing but by 1908 this had been replaced by two longer platforms north of the crossing. Two goods loops were provided but its remote position must have hampered generating much traffic, though in its busiest period, the 1920s, over 9,000 tickets were issued and over 4,000 parcels handled each year. Alongside the first platform was the original station building, with the most elaborate brickwork and bargeboards one could imagine.

The next station is Long Marston, again originally with only a single platform, but subsequently very similar to Milcote. A footbridge between the platforms was added in the 1930s and a small goods yard with a crane and cattle pens was provided. At least the little village was only ½ mile away. South of here we cross the current Gloucestershire border before coming alongside the enormous 1940 Army depot, which covered some 450 acres, with its own interchange sidings and site railway.

The last port of call on the early section of the line is Pebworth Halt, which opened in 1937 though an even smaller halt had existed to the north between 1904 and 1916; Pebworth village was just over a mile away.

Honeybourne junction follows, which was basically a crossroad with our line passing under the Oxford, Worcester & Wolverhampton lines; there were connecting loops on three of the four sides, along with four signal boxes. Honeybourne Junction station was a mile along the OWWR line but it was used as journey's end for many of the stopping trains from Cheltenham.

We are now on the 1904 section, which was built double from the start and eventually had no fewer than eleven stops in its 21 miles. The first is Weston sub Edge, a full mile from its village and, in a desperate attempt to make it sound useful, it bore the prefix 'Bretforton and' for its first three years. Bretforton village

Weston sub Edge in May 1959, with a 9400 series pannier tank heading for Honeybourne, just one year before closure. (Kidderminster Railway Museum)

Broadway station in 1961, looking south towards the goods yard. For many years this was very busy with fruit and vegetable traffic. (Brunel University/Mowat Collection)

is 3 miles away to the north-west! Next came Willersey Halt, only ½ mile from the village, and consisting of two almost identical wooden GWR platforms of the sort normally seen on their own on single branch lines. There were no sidings or facilities.

We now come to the first station of any size, Broadway, which for a short while was the terminus. Though getting on for a mile away, the village was a popular tourist spot and the area is famed for its fruit and vegetable growing. At its peak in the

Stanway Viaduct in happier times. Today it once again carries track and all being well will soon carry steam trains again. (P. Dainty)

1920s over 13,000 tickets were issued, some 22,000 parcels were handled and over 6,000 tons of goods were received. The station was on one side of the road bridge whilst the goods yard, complete with goods shed, crane and cattle pens, was on the other.

Laverton Halt, like Weston, had twin wooden trellis platforms with no facilities beyond the usual pagoda hut on each platform. Between here and Toddington was the viaduct of our earlier sad story, today resplendent with new track, as we shall read later.

Toddington station was the second station of size, with three villages that were all around one mile distant. It had a sizeable goods yard with the normal complement of facilities. There was a large shed, which was used mainly for fruit packing until 1954 when a rail strike turned the growers towards lorries and the roads. A short spur was used for a considerable trade in milk. On race days in Cheltenham the special trains would be stored here whilst their locomotives would go north to turn around on the Honeybourne triangle. Toddington is now flourishing as the HQ of the Gloucestershire Warwickshire Railway.

Next comes Hayles (Hailes) Abbey Halt, opened in 1928, with

Toddington station in the 1960s, showing the massive water tank and the footbridge erected in 1912. (Kidderminster Railway Museum)

Hayles Abbey opened in 1928, with just two small shelters, though it still boasted six trains in each direction into the 1960s. (Kidderminster Railway Museum)

two plain platforms and the little curved corrugated roof huts so common on the GWR rural lines.

Winchcombe is the third station with full facilities, though in the village of Greet; the much larger and beautiful village of Winchcombe is just over a mile away. Like most of the larger stations it had a footbridge between the platforms, and acetylene gas lighting was generated at the station. Next comes the 693-yard-long Greet tunnel at the line's summit.

Gretton Halt was at one end of the little village and again consisted of two GWR wooden trellis platforms with pagoda shelters. Gotherington was another example of a distant village served by a station with a goods yard, double platforms with stone buildings and a signal box, though it was reduced to an unstaffed halt by 1941.

Bishops Cleeve station, at the eastern edge of its sizeable village, was the last full station on our journey. It was provided with a full set of facilities, much of it built with local stone, including the signal box.

Last but not least was Cheltenham Racecourse station, opened

Winchcombe in 1923 on a somewhat dreary day. It was near here that the coal train derailed in 1976, which caused BR to close the line. (Stations UK)

in 1912. It had two shelters, prefabricated at Swindon, a small signal box and at the top of a sloping approach pathway was the wooden booking hall. The station burst into life on race days up to the late 1960s and on occasions up to ten race specials would arrive.

Our arrival in Cheltenham was interrupted by the diminutive High Street Halt, which lasted for nine years from 1908 to 1917. Just 500 yards further on the line joined the much older branch into the St James terminus and continued on to the new Malvern Road station, which opened in 1908, some eighteen months after our line arrived. Many local trains used a short bay platform from which they could reverse back into the St James station to complete their trip. St James was the largest of Cheltenham's stations and the only one near the town centre. It provided four platforms, a coal depot, a large goods shed and sidings and a separate siding into the corporation's central depot. All lasted into the late 1960s but the land, so central to the town, was valuable and as soon as closure was announced it was all demolished, to be replaced by the inevitable office block and, later, a supermarket.

Bishops Cleeve in 1960, with the usual pannier tank and one coach. The main line nature of this route can be seen in many of the photos, with long straight stretches of track. (Kidderminster Railway Museum)

Chetenham Racecourse in 1967, three years after regular passenger trains ended but with still another year or so of use for race meeting specials. (Stations UK)

Cheltenham St James in 1923, the largest and best positioned of all the town's stations. Opened in 1847 it became St James in 1908 and Cheltenham Spa (St James) in 1925. (Stations UK)

Malvern Road was a simpler station with one long central platform reached by a covered walkway from the station buildings. There were passing lines, an engine shed and a simple goods yard. The two road, stone-built engine shed, constructed when the expansion of St James necessitated removing its own shed in 1907, was joined by a second, larger asbestos-clad shed in 1943. Though the line had been built to main line standards, heavy goods trains still needed a banking engine when heading north and these were attached here. Small locomotives that needed turning ran back to St James whilst larger locos used the triangle formed south of the town by the junction with the Andoversford lines.

Early on, steam railcars provided the local services, to be replaced by auto trains in the 1920s. These gave way to diesel railcars, which worked into the 1950s, though pannier tanks were still busy on local services to the end. The relatively limited facilities for steam engines reflects the use of the line as a through route for both goods and passenger trains. Over the years a wide range of GWR types had been seen, along with many intruders from other regions.

Malvern Road station was opened in 1908 and allowed through trains on our line to stop before continuing, without reversing back into St James. Many local services came into the short bay platform and then reversed to St James. (Lens of Sutton Association)

Passenger services were between seven or eight stopping trains per day before the Second World War and between five or six after. A Sunday service ran between the 1920s and 1950s but only consisted of one or two trains. A useful long-distance summer Saturday service carrying holidaymakers started very early, with trains from Birmingham and further north travelling non-stop over our line en route to the West Country. In 1952 when this form of rail travel became extremely popular, three or four of these trains would pass over the line each way, the best known being 'The Cornishman' from Wolverhampton to Penzance, which lasted until 1962. All ran into Cheltenham Malvern Road and many then reversed back into St James.

The line lost its passenger service in 1960 though a parcels service continued. The racecourse station was used until 1968 though the track was left in place until 1976 when, following a derailment, British Rail announced final closure. Immediately the Gloucestershire Warwickshire Railway Society came forward to discuss the possibility of purchasing the line.

The Gloucestershire Warwickshire Railway

Since 1981, much of the Stratford to Cheltenham line has returned to steam operation – currently from Toddington to Cheltenham Racecourse. It is difficult to imagine the state of the line when the agreement to purchase was reached. There was no track, and nearly all the platforms were gone, as were most of the signal boxes and their equipment. The following year the society split into a limited public company and a supporting association. One delightful aspect of the railway's reconstruction is the way that other closed and doomed stations were invaded for items big and small before they too vanished under the bulldozers. The turntable and water tower from Ashford in Kent were early acquisitions, along with the lever frame from Earlswood Lakes. Honeybourne West signal box provided signal posts and another frame. The old signal box at Hall Green was moved brick by brick to Winchcombe in 1986, as was the station building from Monmouth Troy. Later items came from Cardiff Docks, Bristol Harbour and many auctions and swap meets. Platform materials came from Malvern Road, Snow Hill, Broom and Andoversford among other donors. Steam trains ran once again between Toddington and Winchcombe in 1987 – the restoration was under way. In 2003 Cheltenham Racecourse station was reopened and tracks now pass over the Stanway Viaduct and are slowly advancing towards Broadway station. As with other mature heritage railways, a visit today brings about that strange feeling that somehow one has simply slipped back 50 years (full information at www.gwsr.com).

Moreton to Shipston: the branch that time forgot

This remote and long-forgotten line started its life as the Stratford & Moreton Railway which, after some very ambitious

The Gloucestershire Warwickshire Railway today.

(Left) Toddington station, home to the engine works.

Two pictures of Winchcombe, where all the carriage and wagon restoration takes place.

Cheltenham Racecourse station, once again revelling in the sound of steam.

variations, settled down as a tramway between Stratford on Avon and Moreton in Marsh. Its Act was passed in 1821 and the standard gauge, horse-drawn line opened in 1826. It carried passengers but its main purpose was the conveyance of coal from the Stratford Canal to the country villages and the bringing back of stone and agricultural produce to Stratford. Traders using the line provided their own wagons, and passengers had to purchase a monthly licence, which cost the not inconsiderable sum of £1.

Always seen as an extension of the Stratford Canal, the line crossed over the Avon and then divided between lines going around the canal basins (there was a second large basin, long since filled in) and a line for the timber wharf (later a saw mill).

After considerable research by William James, one of the originators of the scheme, the tramway was laid with the very latest track – wrought iron with a wider top section, not unlike normal modern rail. The sections of track had a web that grew deeper towards the centre and became known as fishbelly track. It was held in cast 'chairs', which in turn were nailed into stone blocks. Most tramways of the period used an 'L' shaped track in which the normal wagon wheels of the trucks ran, whereas the fishbelly track provided a supporting surface and the wheels now needed a flange to keep them in place on the rail. All these tramways were horse-drawn and the use of stone blocks to hold the rails allowed the centre of the track to be kept clear for the horses to plod along.

For the first few years the line struggled to make ends meet and, in 1828, a Stratford coal merchant issued a damning report on the state of the line and the problems being met by those who used it. This prompted the board to sack the line supervisor and replace him with John Smith, a friend of Benjamin Baylis who had written the report. Smith quickly rectified the problems and, in 1829, Baylis undertook to rent the line and maintain it. Very soon the line was at last making a small profit, which steadily improved as the years went by until, in 1833, the company felt strong enough to revive its original plan of a branch to Shipston. The Act was duly passed and the branch opened in 1836.

Moreton in Marsh station in 1949, with the branch track just visible on the far right. (R. Carpenter)

Today, the branch is just a short bay platform, with little else left to see. (Author)

Stretton on Fosse was the only other village of any size on the line, seen here in 1930. (Brunel University/Mowat Collection)

During the 1840s the Oxford, Worcester & Wolverhampton Railway evolved but met terrible financial times, which delayed its construction. It had, however, rented the tramway and, in 1853, it brought the line up to standard in anticipation of its own line passing through Moreton in Marsh. Following a disagreement with the GWR, the OWWR turned to the standard gauge London & North Western Company as allies and the line opened in dual gauge in 1853. Our tramway, although still horse-drawn, was now linked to the main railway system.

A twice-daily passenger service was provided using a modified standard railway coach, still horse-drawn. Part of the modification was the provision of a flat wagon onto which the horse would climb in order to ride on the downhill sections – though no doubt enjoyed by the animal, its real use was to prevent the coach running into the horse.

When the Honeybourne to Stratford line opened in 1859 it provided a much better service to Stratford and the tramway was all but abandoned. It was absorbed into the GWR in 1863, who quickly decided that it was better to have a line that lost money than to risk another company entering its territory. The passing loops on the Shipston branch were taken out and the

Longdon Road in 1934, looking clean and ready for traffic with little to suggest its humble origins. (Brunel University/Clinker Collection)

whole line was worked by trains going one way in the morning and the other way in the afternoon.

There was, though, still potential local traffic at the southern end and, in 1882, a seven-year-long rebuilding took place, including a spur where the branch met the Stratford section to enable trains to run without reversing from Shipston to Moreton. In 1889 the track was ready to take steam engines and though the northern section to Stratford quietly rotted away, still with an occasional horse-drawn train, the southern end enjoyed a slow but steady rail service of four trains each way taking around 45 minutes for the journey to Shipston. The stations at Stretton and Longdon Road were built in delightful panelled wood and the gradients on the line were between 1 in 54 and 1 in 68, quite gentle for an ex-tramway, though the original route was laid out by Thomas Telford, which might explain it. There were no signals on the line apart from near Moreton and Shipston, the line being worked with just one engine in steam, which was kept in a small engine shed at Shipston. The early locomotives were 850 class 0-6-0 saddle tanks, which hauled a rather ramshackle selection of coaches. As part of the need for metal in the First World War the section to Stratford was taken up. During 1919, the wartime two trains continued, usually mixed with one bogie coach, plus two or three wagons and a brake van. In 1922 this was increased to three trains. There were just five signals: a home positioned about 200 yards before Shipston station, operated from the platform, plus a down distant; at Moreton there was a down starter, a home and an up distant.

In 1916 the Shipston engine shed was closed and then used by the Army and then as a garage. Passenger trains ended in 1929, with a GWR bus service taking over for a few months, but the passengers didn't come. The line now reverted to a minimum cost goods line bringing mainly coal to both the town's coal merchants but also to the gas works. Hay and livestock were the most common outward traffic. Dean Goods 0-6-0 tender locomotives became the standard type. In the British Railways era there was a short increase in traffic to Shipston; in a good month the line moved over 50 coal wagons plus fertiliser, machinery and miscellaneous goods comprising another 20 or so wagons. Nevertheless that's still only around three wagons for each daily goods train.

The line finally closed in 1960, with the track being lifted over the following three years. Nothing, it seemed, happened fast on this line!

Shipston on Stour terminus in 1934, with a useful looking rake of wagons awaiting their turn in the goods shed. (Brunel University/Clinker Collection)

7
Cheltenham's Long Lost Links, Part 2

Cheltenham–Banbury
Cheltenham–Swindon (MSWJ)
Leckhampton Quarries

Cheltenham–Banbury

Like so many of the longer lines, this one also started with more than one company. The first section was opened from Kingham to Chipping Norton, strictly speaking all within Oxfordshire but important as it made Kingham a junction. The station was known as Chipping Norton Junction until around 1914 when it changed to Kingham. Next came the Bourton on the Water Railway, which obtained its Act in 1860 and just two years later opened its line from the west side of the junction at Kingham, on the still-open Oxford to Worcester line, to Bourton. The first services were worked by two 2-2-2 well tank locos built by Robert Stephenson in 1859 which lasted until 1877. Four trains ran each way between Bourton and Chipping Norton, reversing at the junction.

A scheme was launched to join the Bourton line to Cheltenham, with work starting in 1874 but it was interrupted by the general crisis in the money markets in 1878. Work fortunately restarted in the following year and Cheltenham was reached in 1881. In 1887 the last link between Chipping Norton and Kings Sutton (and thus Banbury) was finished. In 1897 the GWR purchased the line for the bargain price of £138,000. It was logical to run the line as a Cheltenham to Banbury service, particularly as this formed an east–west link of some

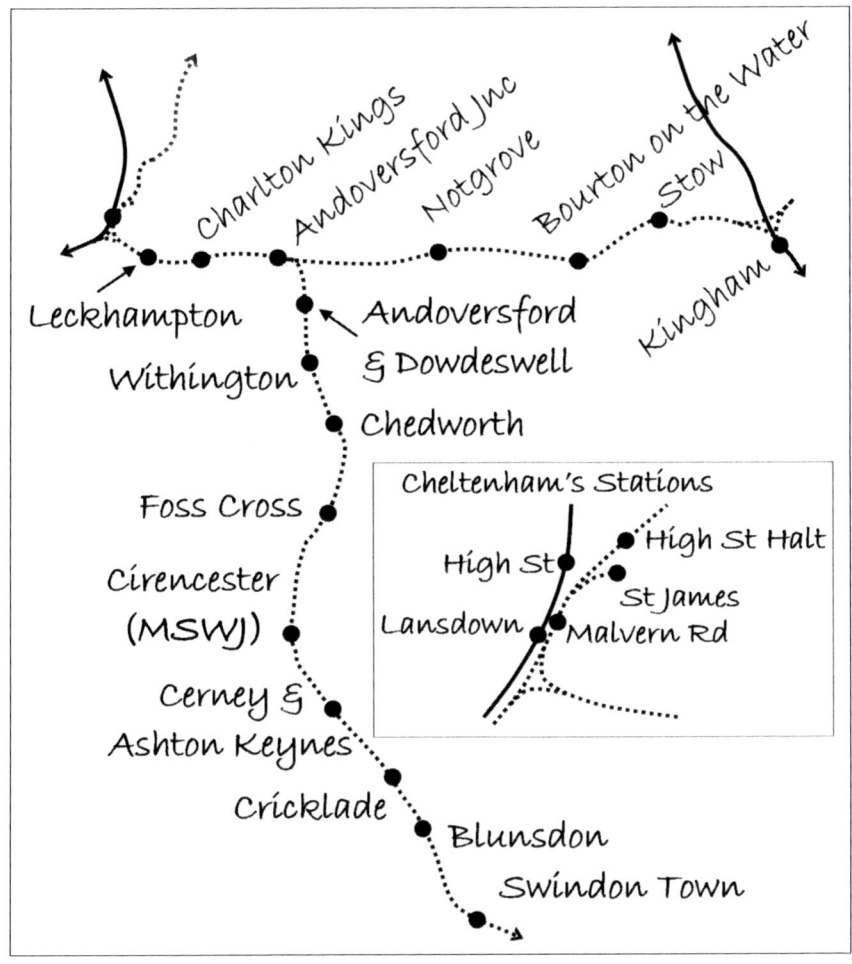

importance. To aid this traffic, a double-track flyover was built in 1906 to enable trains to bypass Kingham without having to go into the station and reverse to continue; this link was reduced to single track in 1958.

The route west from Kingham was just a single line, which climbed at 1 in 38 to Stow, the only station built with a single platform and no passing loop. Unfortunately it was also a full

Kingham station in 1955, looking north towards the junction. Trains for Banbury used the two platforms on the right and, though Cheltenham trains had access to all the platforms, they too usually used the left-hand pair. (Stations UK)

Stow on the Wold station was a long way from the otherwise good-sized village. Perhaps the single platform shows that the builders didn't expect too much. (Lens of Sutton Association)

Bourton on the Water in 1923, with the original station building. (Stations UK)

(Right) The rebuilt station in 1963 after passenger trains had finished. (Author's Collection)

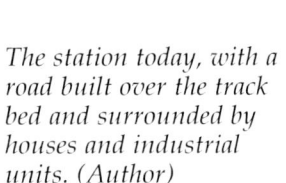

The station today, with a road built over the track bed and surrounded by houses and industrial units. (Author)

mile from the village and some 300 ft lower. The line continued with gradients of 1 in 83 and 1 in 60 to Bourton where a half-timbered station served until rebuilt in Cotswold stone in the 1930s. It had a water tank, cattle pen and a large wooden goods shed, plus four sidings and, for a change, was fairly well placed to serve the village. Notgrove was the summit of the line (also at 760 ft the highest through station on the GWR) though the station was a full 2 miles from the village. It had a passing loop and two platforms. Nevertheless it boasted a full range of facilities, including weighbridge, cattle pen, goods shed and loading crane.

Some more sections of 1 in 60 dropped the line to Andoversford from where further downhill sections took the line into Cheltenham via a tunnel, an impressive viaduct and stations at Charlton Kings and Leckhampton. This last section was doubled in 1902 with connection to the Swindon line, which joined our route at Andoversford.

Some of the through trains were destined for South Wales lines or the Bristol area and needed to turn left at the junction with the main line rather than going north into Cheltenham itself. Such was Cheltenham's reputation that it was felt vital to include its name in the route of these prestigious trains, so the

Notgrove's rather remote station in 1939, with a passenger train heading for Kingham and a goods train facing Cheltenham. (Stations UK)

CHELTENHAM'S LONG LOST LINKS, PART 2

Charlton Kings station in its final year, looking somewhat forlorn. It had become an unstaffed halt at the end of 1956. We are looking towards Kingham and the gradient can be clearly seen. (R. Blencowe)

Leckhampton station in 1923, looking towards Cheltenham. It was renamed 'Cheltenham South & Leckhampton' in 1906 and in 1952 it became 'Cheltenham Leckhampton'. (Stations UK)

little station at Leckhampton, just south of the town, was renamed 'Cheltenham South & Leckhampton' and in 1952 this was shortened to 'Cheltenham Leckhampton'.

Local traffic was for many years handled by the little 517 class 0-4-2 tank engines plus the usual array of GWR prairie tanks, the journey from Banbury to Cheltenham taking 1¼ hours. Both Duke and Bulldog class 4-4-0 locos featured as did the 0-6-0 Dean Goods. By 1902 there were five Chipping Norton to Cheltenham trains, two of which were through trains via Banbury. Interspaced with these was a service of ten trains just between Kingham and Chipping Norton, firstly with steam railcars, later with push-pull sets. By 1944 we were back to just four trains. The line closed to all traffic in 1964.

Cheltenham–Swindon (MSWJ)

Despite the GWR fighting hard to secure its territory, this line managed to not just run through a GWR region but to even penetrate Swindon itself. Worse still, it made friends with the LSWR and the Midland Railway, two GWR rivals, and then had the cheek to remain independent until the 1923 grouping when the GWR had its revenge.

The idea of a line running from Cheltenham to the south coast had been around since the railway mania of the 1840s. The GWR was still firmly broad gauge whilst virtually everyone else used standard gauge. The interchange of goods and passengers between the two gauges was a long-standing problem and one of the scheme's aims was to drive a standard gauge line through GWR territory, allowing trains from the north and the Midlands to reach the south coast uninterrupted. Two early schemes, the Manchester & Southampton Railway and the Manchester, Southampton & Poole Railway, were proposed in the late 1840s but both failed to get their Bill through Parliament. Other schemes appeared and faded, until around 1880 a company called the Swindon, Marlborough & Andover Railway was set up to build a line between Marlborough and Andover. This re-ignited interest in a longer north–south route and prompted

Cheltenham High Street in 1933, showing the sidings and busy goods facilities used by the MSWJ. The station itself had closed in 1917. (Brunel University/Mowat Collection)

the Swindon & Cheltenham Extension Railway, which despite GWR opposition gained its Act in 1883. The company, not unusually, had dreadful financial problems and by the time it had reached Cirencester it was to all purposes completely broke. The extension was worked by the SMA company and within a year the two were joined under the new name – the Midland & South Western Junction Railway. Somehow the company managed to raise a further £200,000 in order to complete the line into Cheltenham, which was ready in 1890. Unfortunately just before the opening a 12-yard section of the brickwork at the southern end of Chedworth tunnel collapsed. Happily, it was repaired but after the inspection 120 yards of embankment slipped as a result of a hard frost and damaged an under-bridge which again needed quick repairs. Following the inevitable high jinks of the GWR over joint running powers on the section from Marlborough, the line opened in 1891. Cheltenham's Lansdown station was extended, and sidings and a goods yard were built adjacent to the Cheltenham High Street station.

In 1892 the LSWR seconded a 36-year-old rising star, Sam Fay,

For many years the MSWJ trains ran from the Midland's Cheltenham Lansdown station, seen here around 1910. The inconveniently placed station still serves the town today. (Kidderminster Railway Museum)

to the MSWJ and he quickly cleared out the somewhat indifferent management and set about getting the new company running properly. He was so successful that it obtained a discharge from receivership in 1897. The short GWR-controlled section was still a thorn in its side and Fay secured a new Bill to permit the building of an independent line so that, by 1898, the MSWJ was in control of its entire route.

Many attempts had been made to link the line to Fairford, where a GWR branch from Oxford terminated, but they all failed, only to be replaced in 1897 by a private venture. This ran a steam-driven van that hauled a 20-seater trailer, plying the roads between Fairford and Cirencester – alas it was not a long-lived enterprise, possibly confirming that a rail link would also have failed.

The line carried vast numbers of troops and supplies from a

branch to Tidworth Barracks and this, plus increased normal traffic, persuaded the board, the Midland and the GWR to double the tracks between Cheltenham and Cirencester in 1902. The line performed sterling work during the First World War, moving vast quantities of goods, including over 6,400 troop trains and 1,400 ambulance trains.

As the map shows, the MSWJ shared the GWR line between Cheltenham and Andoversford Junction but the GWR would not permit MSWJ trains to stop at the junction station; instead they used their own station called Andoversford & Dowdeswell. This somewhat childish action was rescinded in 1904 and after the grouping the GWR closed the Dowdeswell station for passengers in 1927. There were five further stations within Gloucestershire; the first was Withington, built close to the village. The line south of here was doubled in 1902 and the station had two platforms until 1928 when the line was singled. In 1924 the suffix '(Glos)' was added to the name to avoid confusion with a similarly-named station in Herefordshire. There was a small goods yard and a signal box, which lasted until 1956 when the station became unstaffed and it was categorised a halt. Chedworth followed, at first a very simple single platform but rebuilt as a two-platform station when the

Andoversford around 1950, with the line set for the ex-MSWJ line veering to the right. (Kidderminster Railway Museum)

Andoversford & Dowdeswell in 1923. It closed to passengers in 1927 soon after the line became part of the GWR empire, one of the first victims of the 1923 grouping. (Stations UK)

Withington in 1928 when the line was singled. Like many such stations it was downgraded to an unstaffed halt in 1956. (Brunel University/Mowat Collection)

Chedworth in 1935 after the line was singled. The village was originally not served at all, but this station replaced a small wooden structure built to appease the local residents in 1892. (Brunel University/Mowat Collection)

Foss Cross, which, though remote, produced good freight figures. A train prepares to journey south towards Cirencester. (R. Blencowe)

Cirencester station in 1923; it was renamed 'Cirencester Watermoor' a year later. The goods yard and engine shed were to the left behind the station building. (Stations UK)

line was doubled in 1902, complete with a signal box. Once the line had been singled again the signal box closed and, by 1954, it had become an unstaffed halt. Our next station is Foss Cross, built miles from anywhere but fed by two sidings from nearby limestone quarries. Despite its lonely location it had a passing loop with two platforms, plus goods sidings and an engine shed. Though extremely useful for its goods traffic, the passenger figures were always small. By the last years of service, the station was used by just one lady who travelled to and from Cirencester each day.

Next came the largest station on our part of the line – at Cirencester, which was the original headquarters of the MSWJ, resplendent with a locomotive repair works, turntable, goods shed, weighbridge, cattle pens, a wagon repair shop and a siding to the gas works. The water tank was enlarged in 1912 and provided water for the stone-crushing plant at Foss Cross, it being conveyed there in four tank wagons. In 1924 the GWR added the suffix 'Watermoor' to the name to clarify that it had two stations in Cirencester; it also closed down the repair facilities. The signal box closed in 1960 when only one line and platform were used, due to damage by a high vehicle striking a road bridge. Passenger services ended in 1961, with freight lasting until 1964. There had always been fierce rivalry between this station and the Town station (see the next chapter) and despite being on a through route the Watermoor station carried barely half the passenger numbers and even less of the town's goods traffic. As they say today, what's important is the location.

The line south of Cirencester was never doubled and our next station in South Cerney was given a passing loop and two platforms in 1900, at which time it was known as Cerney & Ashton Keynes – always a sign that the nearest inhabitants were a long way away! In fact Cerney was nearly a mile and Ashton was around 4 miles. South Cerney was the largest village in Gloucestershire at one time and the whole area is full of gravel pits, which provided considerable traffic for the line. Though just outside our borders I will mention the next station, Cricklade, as a classic rural station that changed little over the years. Situated on the edge of the village, it boasted a small goods yard and shed, along with two small docks at each end of the station. Goods traffic was dominated by coal coming in and milk going out.

A motley collection of locomotives from several manufacturers pulled trains of old four-wheeled and six-wheeled coaches,

This northerly view of South Cerney (earlier Cerney & Ashton Keynes) taken in 1934 shows the small goods facilities. The signal box was rebuilt in 1942 at this end of the platform. (Brunel University/Mowat Collection)

Cricklade in 1935; the station remained almost unaltered for its entire life and handled useful quantities of freight, including large amounts of milk. (R. Carpenter)

which received virtually no maintenance until Sam Fay had turned the company's fortunes around in 1902. Ex-Midland bogie coaches arrived with electric lighting and steam heating, and better engines led by two 4-4-4 tank engines made by Sharp and Stewart started an era when the line could be proud of its service. The early schedule was usually three passenger trains each way per day but Sam Fay was a stickler for punctual running, which gave rise to complaints from passengers who had become used to the trains turning up 15 or 20 minutes late! By 1913 there were seven trains a day, many coming from the north and going on to the coast.

Goods traffic was always important and produced nearly half the company's revenue, including the output from extensive gravel quarries south of Cirencester, and some 12,000 gallons of milk every day from Cricklade.

In the 1923 grouping nearly all the railway companies in the country were vested in one of the four new companies – the GWR, SR, LMS and the LNER – and it was perhaps inevitable that the MSWJ was placed into the GWR. Initially the line was improved, with repairs and sensible rearrangements being made, but the northern section in Gloucestershire was singled and slowly run down. Blunsdon, which had opened in 1895, was closed, as was Andoversford & Dowdeswell.

Locomotives now included GWR Dukes, 4500s and Dean 0-6-0s. By the 1930s later GWR 2-6-0, 0-6-0 and 2-6-2 locos appeared, plus the occasional class 2800 2-8-0 on heavy freight work. The summers saw visitors such as 'Grange' and 'Manors' and 2-6-0 and T9s from the Southern Railway. The Second World War made good use of this link between the industrial Midlands and the south coast ports but, as was true for so many local lines, the car and lorry were making inroads and when British Railways took over the line it was split between the Western and Southern regions. By 1958 there was only one through service a day and by 1961 it was all over except for a while when the line was used to train drivers on the new DMUs. The line had performed well but it carried terrible debts from the start, from which it never really recovered. The high-ranking shares produced a 2% to 3% return but most normal shares had produced nothing at all.

Leckhampton Quarries

Some 600 ft above Cheltenham is an outcrop of oolitic limestone, which yielded a most useful building stone. Long used, its output was originally brought down by simple horse and cart but around 1800 the new owner of Leckhampton Court laid down a self-acting incline from the quarries to the Birdlip road. Many other inclines followed over the years but they all still needed horse and cart to take the stone into Cheltenham, causing expense and damage. When the Gloucester & Cheltenham Railway (originally a 3 ft 6 in tramway) was formed it included a 2¾-mile branch to meet the inclines, some of which now had three sections. All this tramway network was horse-drawn. As each quarry was worked out the inclines would close; slowly, new quarries were opened, moving eastwards along the ridge towards Hartley Hill, with new inclines being built. During the 1830s some 23,000 tons of stone were supplied and many of Cheltenham's buildings can testify to its fine quality.

In 1922 a new venture was started, primarily to produce lime, and four 70-ft-high kilns were built at the quarry to convert the limestone into lime. A standard gauge railway was built to allow the product to be transferred directly to the main rail network. It commenced with a cable-hauled, self-acting incline about a mile long, which took the trucks down 400 ft, after which the line descended gently to Charlton Kings on the Cheltenham–Banbury line. The work took two years to complete, including a large embankment to carry the incline in a straight and even line, plus a cutting needed to reach the GWR at Charlton Kings. This was cut working towards the GWR and, being downhill, the workface was always wet or flooded, making progress difficult. The incline was fitted with three rails, which widened at the halfway point into four to provide a passing point. The incline was powered from the top with a tension cable that was returned around a pulley at the bottom. The pulley was carried on a trolley which, in turn, was pulled by a cable and balance weight, thus keeping a steady tension throughout. The power was provided by a small generating plant built near Southfield Farm, with duplicated 440-volt alternators turned by a 250 hp gas engine. The output was transformed to 2,200 volts and taken to the quarry where it was transformed back down and

The point where the new line arrived in Charlton Kings with the station in the distance and the interchange sidings on the right. (Author's Collection)

The four lime kilns at the top of the incline, photographed in 1924. The hut between the kilns and the trees was the top of the old tramway 'Middle' incline (H. Household)

used to power the incline, the lights and the fans needed in the kilns.

A lovely little 0-4-0 Peckett saddle tank bought from the Forest of Dean Railway was used to move the trucks over the bottom section and into the exchange siding where GWR locomotives would take the train onto the main network. There were minor runaway accidents but, within the first year, a loaded wagon was allowed to get onto the incline before the haulage cable was attached and, despite all efforts to stop it, it set off down the slope at ever increasing speed. Some say it reached over 100 mph before crashing into two stationary wagons waiting at the incline bottom; all three trucks were ruined, plus the cables were damaged. Some stone (as opposed to lime) was still taken down the incline and a stone yard was set up near Southfield to cut and finish it for building work.

Sadly the venture never took off and, by 1925, the company was in receivership, only to close completely the next year. All the equipment was removed and the lower cutting used for household rubbish infill – a sad end to a long-time local industry.

8
Southern Twigs

Kemble–Cirencester
Kemble–Tetbury
The Fairford branch

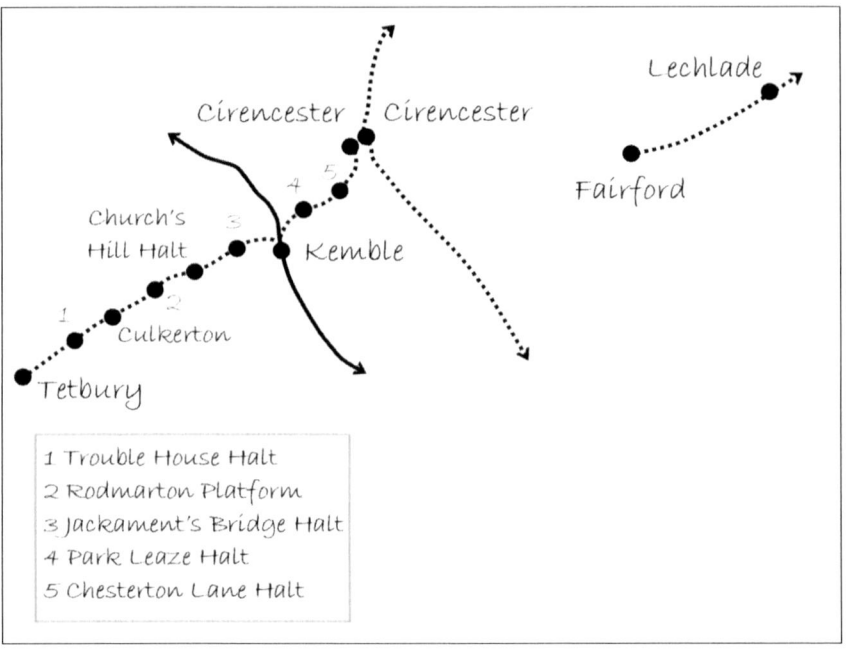

Kemble–Cirencester

Kemble is a small junction station on Brunel's main line from Swindon to Gloucester and Cheltenham, and a branch to Cirencester was included as part of the original plans; in the event the branch was completed before the main line through Sapperton tunnel, and Cirencester served as the terminus for a while.

Cirencester Town station was well positioned near the centre of the town and had an extensive goods yard with some 12 sidings and spurs. There was a sizeable goods shed, rebuilt in 1938, which handled large quantities of bagged fertiliser and animal foodstuff, a large coal yard with four weighing machines, and a cattle pen, which was sited close to the twice-monthly cattle market. An engine shed, rebuilt when the broad gauge was taken up, completed the scene. It was a very busy station in the 1920s, with over 37,000 tickets issued, plus around 50,000 parcels carried. Goods traffic reached over 30,000 tons a year.

The station is a lovely example of Victorian gothic, originally built with an overall roof, as were so many of Brunel's stations, and sympathetically rebuilt in 1956.

The frequency of the train service varied greatly, starting around the six a day level and growing slowly until in the 1900s it was fourteen. This dropped to six again in 1918, recovering to eleven by 1939 with many being mixed. After the war, around

Kemble in 1950, with the still-open main line and the Cirencester branch platform on the right. On the left behind the telegraph pole is the Tetbury platform and signals. (Stations UK)

The Cirencester platform in Kemble station in 1961, with one of the AC railbuses loading parcels. (Author's Collection)

Almost the same view today – now just a siding, and all the platform buildings gone. (Author)

Chesterton Lane Halt in 1960, one of the two tiny platforms built specifically for the little railbuses in an attempt to attract more passengers. (Stations UK)

The approach to the Town station, showing the extensive goods yard. The station was beyond the large goods shed. (Brunel University/Mowat Collection)

Cirencester Town station in 1958, with a class 4500 pannier engine, which would be replaced by the AC railbus service in the following year. This was an experiment by British Railways to see if the fortunes of branch lines could be turned around. (R. Blencowe)

All that is left today is part of the old station building standing in the middle of the 'Old Station Car Park'. The distinctive shape can be seen in both pictures. (Author)

ten trains ran, increasing, after the introduction of a diesel railbus, to around fourteen, with seventeen on Saturdays. Sunday services usually consisted of just two trains but this was increased after 1947 to four until closure.

In 1960 one of the smallest halts ever built was opened at Park Leaze, roughly a mile north of Ewen village. This effort had joined the equally minute halt opened the year before at Chesterton Lane on the southern edge of Cirencester; neither had any buildings or facilities, both being served by the little diesel railbus. As so often happened in the late 1950s and 1960s, usage continued to drop and the passenger service ended in 1964, with goods traffic a year later. Little remains today except part of the Town station; most of the goods yard is now under a supermarket and its car park.

Kemble–Tetbury

Tetbury had been an important town in the wool industry before 1800 and, though this trade started to drop, Tetbury was aggrieved that in 1845 the closest railway was near Kemble. A station had been built on the main line north of the later Kemble station, known as Tetbury Road, which acted as the town's railhead. After the new branch was built it remained as a goods facility, renamed Coates, which lasted in use until 1963.

The town had campaigned for its own line from the 1850s and eventually achieved its line in 1889 after nearly 40 years of waiting, with stations for Culkerton and Tetbury. It was built by the GWR itself rather than by a local company. The branch specialised in halts; the first opened at Rodmarton in 1904 and, being a 'platform' rather than a halt, it had a porter to help passengers and keep things in order. It was one of the standard GWR wooden platforms built on an open trellis-like structure and had one of the lovely little pagoda shelters.

In 1939 Jackament's Bridge Halt was opened to serve those building the nearby Kemble airfield but it closed in 1948 once the hostilities were over. It was a simple open platform with no building or facilities. Culkerton was a proper station, albeit

The Tetbury platform at Kemble today; built much later than the Cirencester branch, it had its own private world feel. (Author)

small. It had a long goods loop and a brick-built goods shed. Culkerton closed to passengers in 1956 when little more than one person a day was using it, but when the railcars arrived in 1959 it was reopened, generating an increase in passengers. It was joined by two further halts – both very simple, low, wooden structures, necessitating the use of steps from the railcars – at Church's Hill Halt and Trouble House, though the latter halt appeared to serve just a pub by the same name. This 17th-century inn had once been called the 'Wagon & Horse' but in times past one of its landlords had hanged himself, whilst a second had drowned. In 1812 it had been the meeting place for rioting farm workers and, on the last day of the passenger service, a rowdy crowd dispatched a coffin full of empty bottles to Dr Beeching, so perhaps its rather odd change of name was justified. (The Trouble House Inn is still there today, looking very smart.)

Rodmarton Platform, opened in 1904, looking back towards Kemble. The spot was remote and exposed, with an unsurfaced track up to the adjacent road with the village still ½ mile away. (Stations UK)

Culkerton station in 1955. This was the the only proper station on the line and had been built with sidings and a goods shed. (Stations UK)

Like the Cirencester branch, the Tetbury line trains were often mixed passenger and goods. This train has stopped by the remains of Culkerton's goods siding. (R. Blencowe)

Tetbury station had a single platform (lengthened in the 1930s to accommodate longer trains carrying strings of polo ponies en route to the Beaufort polo fields at Westonbirt), a goods yard with shed and cattle pen, and a small engine shed. So important was the railway to local farmers that a cattle market was opened next to the station within a year of its opening, with some 120 farmers and dealers in attendance on the first day. It is hard to imagine today but in 1925 over 43,000 milk churns were handled, each holding around 17 gallons of milk. When built the wooden station was actually in Wiltshire but a border alteration put it in Gloucestershire for the greater part of its existence. The station was rebuilt in brick in 1916 as the original wooden structure was in a poor state, despite occasional attempts to repair it. There was a large water tank held aloft by a brick tower at the rear of the engine shed. Prior to 1926 there had been a small signal box at the end of the platform.

Trouble House Halt opened in 1959 for the railbus service. (Stations UK)

A service of around six trains ran for most of the branch's life, propelled by 0-4-2 tank engines, replaced in the last years of steam by pannier tanks. When the AC railbuses arrived, the service increased to eight. A single Sunday train ran between 1910 and 1939 but this was primarily to collect milk. The line closed in 1964, goods traffic having ended the year before; Dr Beeching yet again. It is worth noting that most of these country branches had experienced the effects of the car, lorry and bus for a long time. Tetbury was typical, as the passenger figures show. In 1913 the figure was 17,809, ten years later this had dropped to 14,043 but by 1933 it was a mere 5,895 – that's barely 20 people a day at a time we think of as the pinnacle of the steam network. The line of the railway is still easy to find and the remains of the bay platform at Kemble can be seen. The large cattle pen and goods shed still stand in Tetbury, surrounded by a nicely landscaped car park.

The terminus at Tetbury in 1957; there was a small engine shed, goods shed, crane and cattle pens, all the features of a once busy country station. (Stations UK)

All that remains today, the goods shed and the cattle pens standing unloved in a nicely landscaped car park (Author)

The Fairford branch

This was yet another modest line that was built by two companies. The first, the Witney Railway, following nearly 20 years of debate between the GWR, the London & North Western and the Oxford, Worcester & Wolverhampton companies, opened its line from the Oxford–Worcester main line in 1861. In 1860 the OWWR became part of the West Midland Railway, who agreed to operate the Witney branch. In 1863 the West Midland was swallowed up by the GWR, who now controlled all the lines to the south, west and north of Oxford. In 1861 the East Gloucestershire Railway formed to extend the line from Witney to Cheltenham but, as usual, money proved difficult, though they managed to start work in 1865 at the Cheltenham end. Money, or lack of it, stopped further work and the company decided to concentrate on reaching Fairford first. Intermittent bursts of work followed until the line reached Fairford in 1873. Meanwhile, the little Witney Railway Company had become bankrupt and eventually, in 1890, both companies were absorbed into the GWR. The link between the two lines involved a new station in Witney, the original becoming the goods yard.

Locomotives were a mixed group, including the last single driving wheel locos used on the GWR – two 2-2-2 engines which lasted to 1914. The ever-popular 517 class 0-4-2 tank engines were in use from the late 1800s, plus metro tanks. Later, pannier tanks appeared, along with the occasional 1400 class 0-4-2 tank.

The early Witney line provided four trains daily, which crept up to five, plus one on Sundays, all going through to Fairford by 1910. In the 1930s this was increased with extra trains just serving Witney or Carterton. The latter was opened in 1944 to serve local RAF airfields. After the war, the service peaked with six Fairford trains, plus two to Carterton and two on Sundays. As the car, lorry and bus took hold of traffic during the 1950s, the service was reduced back to four trains and no Sunday service and, by 1962, all passenger services ended, leaving a meagre goods service as far as Witney. This depended on diesels after 1965 when the last steam engine ran, but even this usage

A classic country station – this is Lechlade in 1958, all spruce and tidy but alas devoid of passengers. (Stations UK)

ended in 1970, leaving the line to join so many of its neighbours in gentle decay. Today, much of the line has been used for modern road building.

The line was used in 1906 for trials of the GWR Automatic Train Control System, which used a ramp in the centre of the track to convey the danger if the driver passed a signal at red and so apply the train's brakes.

The traffic was mainly agricultural except for the early carriage of coal to the Witney woollen mills, who could now install steam engines to power the looms and thus make their main product, blankets, competitive once more.

The line saw a massive increase in traffic around the Witney end during the Second World War as airfields were constructed on the flat land, bringing materials, men and armaments in by rail.

The only two stations within Gloucestershire were Lechlade and Fairford. Lechlade was ½ mile from the town and the station handled a lot of goods traffic, peaking some years at over 10,000 tons. Like Fairford, the station was a neat affair built in the local Cotswold stone, with a small signal box on the platform and a stone-built goods shed.

Fairford had all the marks of a through station and had been built when the original company still had hopes of reaching Cheltenham; therefore its position and layout made for a very poor terminus. It had a single platform and though passengers could alight from long excursion trains there was insufficient room for the engine to run around the train in order to haul the train back. Instead, the train was pulled forward into the goods loop, and the engine was detached and positioned on the adjacent track, from where it hauled the coaches back towards the buffers, using a cable, until the points were cleared, allowing the engine to regain its position. The line at this end was prone to flooding in times of heavy rain and the trackbed suffered from instability. Fairford also contributed large quantities of traffic, mostly milk for London, which peaked at 15,000 gallons a day! As the station was over one mile from the town, which only had around 1,400 inhabitants, it is not surprising that passenger traffic was always sparse. Beyond the goods yard was a water tank (fed from a well, using a pump driven by steam taken from a locomotive), an engine shed and a small turntable.

The terminus at Fairford in 1958. The goods shed can be seen with the rest of the sidings and the engine shed beyond, giving the normal layout for a through station – compare with Lechlade. To operate as a terminus was always awkward. (Stations UK)

9
The Midland Railway's Branches

The Nailsworth branch
The Stroud branch
The Dursley branch
Sharpness and the Severn Bridge
The Thornbury branch

The Nailsworth branch

This line was opened very quietly in 1867 by the Stonehouse & Nailsworth Railway Company and was vested in the Midland Railway in 1878, with the original company being dissolved in 1886. Its primary use was to take coal to the many mills along the valley, many of which had started with a water wheel driving the machinery but were now being converted to steam engines to increase production.

Stonehouse Bristol Road station in 1932 with the main line on the right and the branch line leaving to the left. (Brunel University/Mowat Collection)

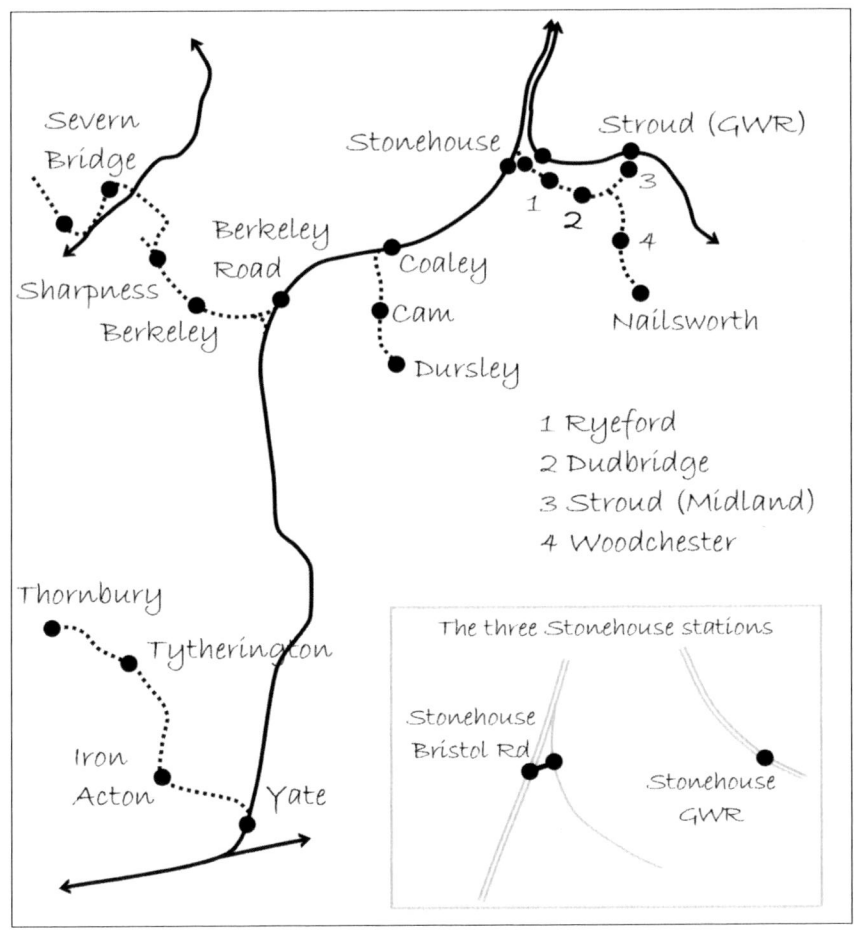

The branch had a passenger service of four trains when it opened, which climbed to seven by 1890, to nine by 1910, dropping to seven in 1930 and back up to eight after the war. Steam railcars were used extensively in the area from around 1900 but they were not popular with either the crews or the passengers and were slowly replaced in the 1920s by push-pull auto sets. These survived on the branch into the late 1950s before giving way to diesel railcars.

Stonehouse station on the Nailsworth branch in 1923. The station closed in 1947. (Stations UK)

The branch left the main line at Stonehouse (Bristol Road), which had a slightly unusual layout. There were platforms for both the main line and the branch but both were over ¼ mile down their respective lines from the actual junction, the space between being a goods yard with a goods shed, cattle pens and,

Today all that remains of the entire complex is the stationmaster's house. (Author)

until 1934, a turntable. After closure this area was used as a coal concentration depot until 1989. The Nailsworth platform was fed by a long footbridge from the car park of the main line station but ceased to be used after 1947.

The line set off in an easterly direction running parallel to the Stroudwater Canal and after barely ½ mile there was a short siding to the Stonehouse wharf to permit exchange of goods. The first station was Ryeford which, though only a single platform station, had two important private sidings. One fed saw mills immediately to the north of the station and was rail connected for nearly 100 years, the other was the Stanley Woollen Mills, rail connected until 1930.

Dudbridge followed and was a full-sized station with two platforms and two long sidings following the opening of the Stroud branch. From one of these sidings a short private siding served a local flour mill. All the lines including the station itself were singled in 1957. All the stations served their own close but small villages on the southern side of the valley but the GWR main line on the northern side served two bigger villages at Stonehouse and Ebley.

The next station was Woodchester, provided with a single

Ryeford station in 1932, showing the goods shed and on the left part of the saw mills. There appears to be just one passenger waiting. (Brunel University/Mowat Collection)

Dudbridge in 1923, looking back towards Stonehouse. This was the only passing loop on the branch; unfortunately the handsome station building was demolished in the 1970s. (Stations UK)

Just south of the station was the junction for the Stroud branch, with the Nailsworth line continuing straight on, taken in 1955. (Kidderminster Railway Museum)

Woodchester station in 1932. The little signal box controlled the crossing gates and the local signals. (Kidderminster Railway Museum)

platform and level crossing, after which came the quite substantial goods yard from the rear of which was yet another private siding, into Henry Workman's saw mill, active until 1964.

Barely 6 miles after leaving the main line and still confined by the narrow valley, the line reached Nailsworth. The station had a single platform with a run round loop, plus a turntable and engine shed, all built on an embankment, with ideas that the line might be extended to Tetbury. Nearly ¼ mile before the station buffers a line serving the goods yard left and descended to the natural ground level. The yard had a weighing machine, five sidings and a goods shed. Perhaps the over optimism of the early company can be gauged when we note that the signal box closed in 1886, the engine shed in 1895 and the turntable in 1920. The station building was a very impressive structure and with a local population of around 3,000 presumably passenger traffic was expected to be good. The first passenger service provided just four trains but this slowly grew as the years went by until an eight-train service was introduced in 1946. However, this must have failed to attract business as passenger services ended the following year, with freight carrying on until June 1966.

A lovely postcard view of Nailsworth station from 1912. Now it is a private house with no trace of the line. (Lens of Sutton Association)

The goods facilities were lower than the station but only this warehouse remains today. (Author)

On the approach road the station hotel still stands today. (Author)

The Stroud branch

The 1-mile-long branch from Dudbridge to Stroud was opened to goods traffic in 1886 after construction that took three years, mainly due to the need for a 145-yard curved viaduct. Originally it was to share the GWR station but this idea failed and its own station was built close by but on the other side of the Thames & Severn Canal. On the approach to the town a coal siding had been built in 1921 to exchange coal into a 2 ft gauge railway that crossed over the river Frome and served the gas works, which had previously used the canal. Some 3,000 tons of coal were supplied each month until 1958.

Passenger services started at Dudbridge on the Nailsworth line and most connected with the Nailsworth trains. There were a few trains that reversed at Dudbridge, providing a Nailsworth to Stroud link. The station was controlled by two ground frames and never had a signal box. Passengers tended to find the GWR station more convenient and the line closed to passengers in 1947, after which it relied on its goods traffic to justify its existence. In latter years Midland 3F engines handled most of

Stroud Wallgate in 1932, showing the timber-built station with the goods yard beyond. This had a large timber yard, goods shed, crane and cattle pens and indeed kept the line going long after passenger services ended. (Brunel University/Mowat Collection)

Just for interest, the ex-GWR station next door in 1964, which always provided a better passenger service and still does today. (Stations UK)

the traffic and in BR days class 2s appeared until the goods traffic ended in 1966.

The Dursley branch

This little branch was built by the Dursley & Midland Junction Railway and opened in 1856; it was taken over by the Midland Railway five years later. Just 2½ miles long, it had seven private sidings and was always busy with goods traffic, principally bulk grain, paper, agricultural machinery and coal. The line left the main line at Coaley, a conventional junction with the branch turning south along its own platform. The small station building sat across the platforms at a right angle to the main line. There were sidings to the south of the platform that stretched back alongside the main line to the cattle pens, which must have caused consternation when an express passed by! To the other side of the branch line was a goods shed and further sidings, which gave the strange appearance of the branch train leaving by passing through the middle of the goods yard. Today the modern

Cam & Dursley station sits roughly where the cattle pens had been, opened in 1994 on the main line as a park & ride facility.

The only intermediate station was at Cam, a small platform completely overpowered by the woollen mill that lay alongside. The little goods shed was fed by a tramway siding, which vanished into the depths of the mill and presumably only handled smaller packages for the mill. The mill had its own normal sidings, which were used until the late 1950s, and there was a small public goods siding, which lasted until 1964. The little level crossing was protected by signals that were all operated from a small signal box but there was no conventional signalling as the line always worked on the 'one engine in steam' principle.

On the approach to Dursley was the local gas works, to which the line conveyed around 4,500 tons of coal annually until 1948 and, in a somewhat lonely spot, the engine shed on a very short spur. The water tank for the locomotives stood the other side of the line. Dursley station had a single, slightly curved platform

Coaley junction in 1956, with a more conventional layout. The station building stood across the platforms, having been built by the Dursley company. (Kidderminster Railway Museum)

Cam & Dursley park & ride today. The old branch left roughly where the dumped car sits. (Author)

Cam station in 1962, looking towards Dursley. The chimneys belong to the massive woollen mill. (Lens of Sutton Association)

Possibly one of the earliest railway postcards of Dursley station in 1866. (Author's Collection)

A similar shot taken in 1912, with a somewhat more modern engine approaching. (Lens of Sutton Association)

tucked away in the corner of a fairly large goods yard. The platform was dominated by factories, including those of R.A. Lister, manufacturers of petrol and diesel engines and agricultural machinery, who had their own sidings.

Two Johnson 1F 0-6-0 tank engines worked the line for many years up to 1960, aided by the occasional pannier tank. The passenger train was known as the 'Dursley Donkey' almost from the opening; it had just one coach except on Saturdays when two were provided. The train often worked mixed, with a van or two attached to the coach. It ran six trips a day, which rose during the 1920s and 1930s to seven or eight, the trip taking nine minutes. Like so many branch lines, the passenger figures dropped steadily after 1950 and the line closed to passengers in 1962, with public goods traffic lasting until 1968. The entire line then operated as a private siding just serving Lister's for a further two years, after which the factory was extended across the goods yard area and swallowed up the station as well. A case of biting off the hand that fed you!

Sharpness and the Severn Bridge

Crossing the River Severn below Gloucester had long occupied the attention of speculators from the very first days of railway construction in the area. All schemes had failed bar one that proposed a tunnel, which was actually started but a disastrous leak brought the work and the idea to an abrupt end. By 1844 Brunel was engaged in surveying the route for the South Wales line and, as the main route from London was in construction down the Golden Valley and into Stroud, it seemed logical to continue straight across the Severn and thus gain access to the northern shoreline and on to South Wales. He proposed a massive bridge plus a branch to Hereford but the Admiralty would have nothing of the sort. A second revised scheme met the same rebuff, plus the good people of Gloucester were none too pleased to be left out of such a potentially important line. A third scheme for a 1½-mile tunnel also failed and the route was changed to the one we still have today via Gloucester.

Ever more adventurous schemes continued to be proposed, all failing, until in 1871 no fewer than six new ideas were put forward. Two of these, a tunnel just 8 miles north of Bristol and the 'Severn Bridge Railway No 2 (Sharpness)', passed through Parliament and obtained their Bills.

Our story involves the latter scheme – a line built from Berkeley Road junction on the Midland main line to Sharpness and then extended over the bridge and taken on to join the Severn & Wye Railway at Lydney. The first section to the then embryo port at Sharpness was opened by the Midland Railway to goods traffic in 1875. Berkeley Road station was one of the original Brunel broad gauge stations opened in 1844 with the Bristol to Gloucester line. When the branch was built it was given its own pair of platforms to the west of the main line ones. The only intermediate station on the branch was Berkeley and, though a mile from the village, the typical Midland station had two platforms, a small goods yard with a goods shed and a little signal box. Sharpness started with a temporary station adjacent to the new docks but plans for the bridge were already well

Berkeley Road station, with the Sharpness branch veering off to the right. All four lines had platforms, reflecting the high hopes in 1875 when it was opened. (Kidderminster Railway Museum)

Berkeley station in 1912, still with double track (until 1931) and a busy goods yard. Main line trains to South Wales were often diverted through here on Sundays when maintenance work was being carried out on the Severn tunnel. (Lens of Sutton Association)

Today, in a corner of what was the Berkeley goods yard, this gantry was built to transfer nuclear waste from lorries to rail, though now only occasionally used. (Author)

A 1950 view of Sharpness station, with some of the dockside buildings in the background. The railcar was on charter to the Birmingham Locomotive Club. (Lens of Sutton Association)

under way and, just three years later, a new brick station was opened and the early site closed. As with so many branch line stations there was one station building, inevitably single storey, with a simple shelter on the other platform. These station buildings often had no doors in the rear wall; passengers gained access to the platform via a gate in the fence and then walked into the booking office from the platform. Despite reasonable levels of goods traffic the line was singled in 1931, with all three stations reverting to using the platform that had the station building.

It was hoped that both the Midland and the GWR would take an active part in the bridge project but, in the event, the GWR declined to go beyond paying the minimum sum (£25,000) to ensure it had running rights over the route. The Midland at least paid twice that sum and took a more encouraging stance. The bridge was expected to cost around £300,000, though, interestingly, the GWR tunnel further south was estimated at £1 million.

Even in the 1870s this was still a major project; the River Severn is a dangerous and at times furious beast, as the contractors were soon to discover. After a slow start, work commenced in July 1875.

The bridge company were in a peculiar position as they had no traffic of their own and depended entirely on the Midland and, more importantly, the Severn & Wye Company for any profit. Thus it made sense for the bridge company and the Severn & Wye to join forces and the two amalgamated in 1878.

The line was to continue from the Sharpness station, turn north-west and cross the river, then on reaching the northern bank to turn again south-west and descend to Lydney, and thus to the lines from the Forest of Dean coal and iron areas. There was also a link to the GWR South Wales line to enable the GWR to use its rights over the route. The bridge itself consisted of a 200-ft-long swing bridge that crossed over the Gloucester & Sharpness Canal and then continued with 21 fixed spans (14 at 134 ft, 5 at 174 ft and 2 at 312 ft). The two larger spans formed the navigation channel for craft using the river and were held aloft on piers formed from four cast-iron cylinders, all others

Even though rail traffic has ceased, the tracks still remain all around the docks. This is the swing bridge that carried the north docks branch. (Author)

The Severn bridge in 1912, with the canal nearest the camera and the fateful arches in the far distance. (Lens of Sutton Association)

being just two cylinders. The cylinders were filled with concrete once they were in place. The last section over the shallow northern shoreline was formed by a conventional stone viaduct, which completed the ¾-mile-long structure. The swing bridge was built to take two tracks but only ever had a single track on it. It was swung by power from a pair of steam engines housed in the base of the tower and had a fireman and engine driver as its staff.

Almost immediately after the viaduct, the line doubled for the somewhat remote Severn Bridge station, returned to a single line to plunge into a 506-yard tunnel and then started its 3-mile descent towards Lydney. A new junction station was built, plus a considerable goods yard and loco depot. At Sharpness a branch was built to serve the northern side of the new docks, crossing the dock on a second swing bridge. The Severn bridge opened for public services in October 1879 but alas the high hopes for traffic failed to materialise. The Forest of Dean coal industry had peaked in the early 1800s and was now in serious decline; the iron industry had been hampered because the type of iron produced was unsuitable for making steel in the

Severn Bridge station viewed from above the tunnel entrance during the 1960s, with the tracks slowly rusting. (J. Norton)

Bessemer converters and the world now wanted steel. The GWR, who had taken some of their South Wales coal over the bridge, quite naturally reverted to using their new tunnel as soon as it was completed. Things got steadily worse until, in 1894, the line was purchased jointly by the Midland and GWR and became simply the Severn & Wye Joint Railway.

In 1932 a scheme to deck the bridge at rail level, rather like a continuous level crossing, so that vehicles could use the bridge in between the infrequent trains, was proposed but not implemented.

In British Railways' times the bridge was repainted and improved. Tests were undertaken to see if the weight limitations could be increased to allow heavier engines to cross; after extensive measurements it was found that the diagonal members were the problem and so a contract was drawn up to replace all 488 links in 1960.

Though the bridge had been struck by boats several times over the years none had been serious, but that was to change on 25th October 1960. It was a foggy evening and two oil tankers had missed the turn for the Sharpness dock, struck each other and then drifted as a pair northwards, carried by the mischievous tide, until they hit pier 17 of the bridge. The impact brought down two spans of the bridge and caused a massive explosion, covering the river in blazing oil. Only one member of the two crews survived. The event could have been much worse as the work teams replacing the diagonal members of the spans would normally have been working on the very spans that fell; instead they had taken an early meal break at the bridge station to listen to the Henry Cooper v Karl Muller boxing match on the radio.

British Railways prepared designs and estimates to repair the bridge but, as if the Gods were trying to send a message, the bridge was stuck again only five months later by the *BP Explorer*. The tanker had capsized and was drifting in the tidal currents, having passed through the navigation channel, and then when the tide turned it drifted back, striking pier 20. All the crew were drowned though just why the vessel capsized was never fully explained. As part of the recovery of the fallen spans, a twin floating crane was brought down from Liverpool with the lovely name of 'Tweedledum & Tweedledee' but this too managed to hit the bridge at pier 20, damaging the protective 'dolphins' around the pier and, to add insult to injury, its jib also hit the railway span above!

The costs of the repairs were now estimated at £¼ million and, with the tunnel just 14 miles away and no inter-company rivalry to blur the decision making, the bridge's fate was sealed. By 1970 the structure had been completely removed though, as the ten year gap suggests, the work was not easy or well organised.

With the bridge unusable, the line beyond Sharpness closed to Lydney on 25th October 1960, and to Sharpness in 1964. A small loading depot was built at Berkeley to handle waste from the Berkeley atomic power station and, though the track is still in place to Sharpness, only the occasional freight train runs, the line being operated as a private siding. Both approach lines to the bridge have since disappeared, including Severn Bridge station. The stone tower of the swing bridge over the Gloucester & Sharpness Canal still stands, though I suspect most boaters and walkers have no idea of its history.

The Thornbury branch

The Thornbury branch opened to passengers in September 1872, leaving the main line at the north end of Yate station. Its single line curved sharp left and headed west for 2 miles to reach Iron Acton. Here a short branch headed south to iron ore quarries near Frampton Cotterell in 1868 but, within a couple of years, the pit was exhausted. The Frampton branch track was eventually lifted in 1892 but relaid in 1902 to carry stone traffic, which lasted just five more years. After that, only a short section of track remained, being used for local goods.

The Thornbury line continued on through Iron Acton station, which had a surprisingly large building, turned gently north and then north-west to reach Tytherington station after climbing at 1 in 61. This station had just a single platform with a very modest building but it heralded the start of the sidings into the two large quarries. On the right was the Church Quarry, which worked from 1898 to around 1944, and to the left was West Quarry, active from 1895 to 1963. Ahead lay the first of two short tunnels, then the 224-yard-long Tytherington tunnel over which the M5 passes today and so to the sidings feeding the Grovesend Quarry, which worked from 1888 to 1967. In 1972 this quarry was restarted and the branch line relaid. Though rail conveyance stopped in 1990 the track is still in place with signs of occasional use.

Yate station in 1962, looking south. The Thornbury branch left a few hundred yards north. (Stations UK)

Iron Acton station under invasion from railway enthusiasts in 1956. The platform was on the left and the station building can be seen just behind the pannier locomotive. (Stations UK)

Next came the 167-yard Grovesend tunnel and the final mile descent into Thornbury, where a single platform boasted a rather fine Midland-style station building. All the basic rural facilities were provided: cattle pens, goods shed, sidings, engine shed and a turntable, which survived in use until 1957 long after passenger trains had ceased in 1944.

This might be a fitting moment to describe just how important these early branch lines were to the local population. On the first day of traffic the Mayor travelled from Bristol on the first train and was greeted at Thornbury by a brass band and then taken to

Tytherington station in 1932 near the end of the gruelling 1 in 61 climb; it heralded the start of the quarries. (Brunel University/Mowat Collection)

the Swan Hotel where the local dignitaries and people celebrated. The town's streets had been decorated with flags and arches, the parish bells were rung and the shops closed soon after 11 am for the rest of the day. Over 700 children and their teachers took a trip to Yate paid for by public subscription, and arriving back were provided with a substantial tea in a local field. As so often, disquiet was voiced in the local paper at the length of the journey to Bristol. Locals had long used road transport to Patchway station (quite close to the present day park & ride station) and thence into Bristol – shorter, quicker and cheaper.

Passenger trains, usually hauled by 0-6-0 tender locomotives, ran initially just twice a day to Yate. This soon improved, with most going to Bristol, forming a suburban service to the Midland stations in the north of the city. By the early 1940s passenger numbers were painfully low, typically averaging around 20 per day, and the closure to passengers in 1944 was hardly a surprise. Goods traffic, always busy, ended in 1967, having enjoyed a brief revival in the early 1960s with materials for the first Severn road bridge and the Oldbury-on-Severn nuclear power station. Today Thornbury station site is completely gone, covered by a supermarket. Thornbury enjoyed brief fame back in 1885 when a stranded whale was beached at Littleton some 4 miles away. Around 40,000 visitors came by rail to see the sight, many walking to Littleton.

The enthusiasts' train (seen in the picture on page 153) at the terminus, Thornbury. The delightful station building was still standing in 1956 to watch over the occasional goods traffic. (Stations UK)

Conclusion

Gloucestershire's railways covered the entire spectrum from famously fast trains to lazy branch lines, some barely a mile in length. The materials produced and moved within its borders were also very varied, including coal, iron, timber, limestone and a wide range of dairy and farm produce, yet none brought fame or fortune. Like many English counties, Gloucestershire quietly got on with life whilst vast quantities of people and goods rumbled through its railway system, just as the motorways do now.

Today there is just one main line, three busy minor lines and eight stations, all that is left of a network that once covered some 250 route miles and had over 140 stations. These figures help us to realise how great a change has occurred and how considerable effort is needed to imagine what life was like just 50 or 60 years ago when all but two of the lines featured in this book were still open.

It is very easy for the enthusiast to become excessively sentimental and to complain at the way our railway system was savagely reduced in the 1960s. If we are honest, though, the signs of the losing battle go back to the 1920s, and by the 1930s the decline in passenger traffic was in full swing. It is ironic that today the crowded roads are making our existing lines busier than ever and that undoubtedly many of the closed lines would now be viable again.

In searching out old routes I have become ever more aware of just how completely their tracks have been covered. Traces of old railway features could be easily found even just 10 or 20 years ago but, today, the pace of redevelopment is so fast and widespread that one finds it hard to believe that some of the railways ever existed.

Hopefully this book will help hold the past in suspension and give a glimpse of these long-vanished features. Thankfully we also have the work of the enthusiasts who have created the preserved railways, still working, with real steam engines providing the sounds and smells of a bygone era. Gloucestershire has two excellent examples, both of which I urge you to visit to experience that strange time-warp feeling of being back in the 1930s.

Opening and Final Closure Dates of Lines to Regular Passenger Traffic

Line	Opened	Final Closure
Moreton/Shipston	5.9.1826	8.7.1929
Kemble/Cirencester	31.5.1841	6.4.1964
Gloucester/Ross on Wye	2.6.1855	2.11.1964
Coaley/Dursley	18.9.1856	10.9.1962
Ashchurch/Malvern	16.5.1864	14.8.1981
Ashchurch/Evesham	1.10.1864	1.7.1963
Stonehouse/Nailsworth	4.2.1867	16.6.1947*
Yate/Thornbury	2.9.1872	19.6.1944
Witney/Fairford	15.1.1873	18.6.1962
Monmouth/Ross on Wye	4.8.1873	5.1.1959
Lydney/Lydbrook Junction	23.9.1875	8.7.1929
Lydney/Coleford	9.12.1875	8.7.1929
Berkeley Road/Sharpness	1.8.1876	2.11.1964
Monmouth/Chepstow	1.11.1876	5.1.1959
Lydney/Cinderford	5.8.1878	6.7.1929
Sharpness/Lydney Junction	17.10.1879	25.10.1960
Cheltenham/Banbury	1.6.1881	15.10.1962
Monmouth/Coleford	1.9.1883	1.1.1917
Cheltenham/Swindon (MSWJ)	18.12.1883	11.9.1961
Gloucester/Ledbury	27.7.1885	13.7.1959
Dudbridge/Stroud	1.7.1886	16.6.1947*
Kemble/Tetbury	2.12.1889	6.4.1964
Cheltenham/Stratford on Avon	1.6.1906	7.3.1960
Gloucester/Cinderford	3.8.1907	3.11.1958

* Date of last passenger train, official closure date was later.

Nearly all lines carried goods traffic after the passenger services ended, in some cases for 30 or 40 more years, and several opened for goods traffic a year or two before the passenger services started.

One or two sections of line continued in use as private sidings beyond the public goods closure.

Bibliography

Along with many hours poring over old maps, a great many publications were consulted in the writing of this book, a number long out of print. Those listed below are believed to still be in print or at least are easy to find secondhand.

Edwards, Dennis & Pigram, Ron *Cotswold Memories* (Greenwich Editions)
Glover, Celia *The Ross and Monmouth Railway* (Brewin Books)
Handley, B.M. & Dingwall, R. *The Wye Valley Railway* (The Oakwood Press)
Huxley, Ron *The Severn Bridge Railway 1872–1970* (Alan Sutton)
Jenkins, S.C. & Carpenter, R.S. *The Shipston on Stour Branch* (Wild Swan Publications)
Maggs, Colin *Railways of the Cotswolds* (Peter Nicholson)
Mitchell, Vic & Smith, Keith *Branch Line Series* (Middleton Press)
Mourton, Stephen *Steam Routes Around Gloucester* (Runpast Publishing)
Oakley, Mike *Gloucestershire Railway Stations* (The Dovecote Press)
Russell, J.H. *The Banbury and Cheltenham Railway 1887–1962* (Oxford Publishing Co)

Photographs

For those who would like to obtain photographs of their own, the following four libraries may be of interest:

Brunel University Collections, 3 Fairway, Clifton, York YO30 5QA
Kidderminster Railway Museum, Station Approach, Comberton Hill, Kidderminster DY10 1QX
Lens of Sutton Association, 46 Edenhurst Road, Longbridge B31 4PQ
Stations UK, PO Box 462, Southport, Merseyside PR8 3WA

INDEX

Andoversford 91, 93, 104, 109
   Junction 109
   & Dowdeswell 109, 110, 115
Ashchurch 10–17
Ashton 16, 17
Awre 46

Banbury 100–106, 116
Barbers Bridge 55, 57, 59
Beckford 16, 17
Bengeworth 16
Berkeley 145, 146, 151
Berkeley Road 145
Bilson Halt 35, 37
Birmingham & Gloucester Railway 9, 11, 19, 21
Bishops Cleeve 88, 90
Blaisdon Halt 62, 63
Blakeney 46
Blunsdon 115
Bourton on the Water 100, 103, 104
   Railway 100
Bretforton 85
Bristol 8, 9, 25, 28, 74, 93, 104, 145, 153, 154
Bristol & Gloucester line 9, 19
Broadway 82, 86–87, 93
Brockweir Halt 81
Bullo Cross Halt 32
Bullo Pill 30 *seq*

Cam 141, 142
Cam & Dursley 141, 142
Carterton 129
Cerney & Ashton Keynes 113
Charlton Kings 104, 105, 116
Chedworth 109, 111, 112
Cheltenham 8, 10, 16, 17, 24, 82–117, 118, 129, 131
   'Flyer' 28
   High Street Halt 85, 107
   Lansdown 107, 108

'Link' 19, 21
Malvern Road 89, 91, 92, 93
Racecourse 88 *seq*
St James 89, 91, 92
Spa 91, 92
Chepstow 9, 28, 74–81
Chesterton Lane Halt 121, 123
Chipping Norton 100, 106
Church's Hill Halt 124
Cinderford 28, 30–46, 71
Cirencester 107 *seq*, 118–123
   Town 113, 119, 121, 122
   Watermoor 112, 113
Coaley 140, 141
Coleford 38, 39, 42, 46–51
   Railway 47
   Railway Museum 51
Coleford, Monmouth, Usk & Pontypool Railway 47
Cricklade 113–114
Culkerton 123 *seq*

'Daffodil Line' 53–59
Dean Forest Railway 41, 42, 51–52
Drybrook 30 *seq*, 64
Drybrook Road 31, 42, 44
Dudbridge 135, 136, 140
Dursley 28, 140–144
Dursley & Midland Junction Railway 140
Dymock 54, 57, 58

East Gloucestershire Railway 129
Evesham 16–17

Fairford 108, 129–131
Forest of Dean 8, 28, 30–52
Forest of Dean Central Railway 46, 117
Foss Cross 111, 112
Four Oaks 55, 57

INDEX

Gloucester 8, 9, 11, 16, 18–29, 38, 44, 53–65, 68, 74, 82, 118, 144
    Central 24, 25
    Eastgate 21, 23, 24, 25
    Midland 21, 22, 23
    'T' station 19
Gloucester & Cheltenham Railway 115
Gloucestershire Warwickshire Railway 87, 92, 93, 94
Gotherington 88
Grange Court 30, 60 *seq*
Great Western Railway 9, 16, 19 *seq*, 30 *seq*, 54 *seq*, 66 *seq*, 82 *seq*, 100 *seq*, 123, 129, 135, 139, 140, 147, 148, 150
Greenway Halt 57
Gretton 88

Hadnock Halt 73
Hayles Abbey Halt 87, 88
Hereford 8, 54, 59, 63, 65, 74, 144
Hereford, Ross & Gloucester Railway 66
Hinton 16, 17
Honeybourne 17, 82 seq, 97
    Junction 84, 85
    West 93
Howbeach Slade 46

Iron Acton 152, 153

Jackament's Bridge Halt 123

Kemble 118–128
Kerne Bridge 69, 70, 73
Kingham 100 *seq*
Kings Sutton 100

Laverton 83, 87
Lechlade 8, 130, 131
Leckhampton 104, 105, 106
Leckhampton Quarries 115–117
Ledbury 53–59
    Town 57
Llandogo Halt 81
London & North Eastern Railway 114

London & North Western Railway 97, 129
London & South Western Railway 106, 107
London, Midland & Scottish Railway 114
Longdon Road 98
Longhope 62, 63
Long Marston 85
Lydbrook 30 *seq*, 66 *seq*
    Junction 44, 46, 69, 71
    Lower 44, 45
    Upper 44. 45
    Viaduct 46
Lydney 30 *seq*, 145, 148, 151
    Junction 38, 40, 41
    Town 40, 41

Malswick 57
Malvern 10–14
Manchester & Southampton Railway 106
Manchester, Southampton & Poole Railway 106
Midland & South Western Junction Railway 106–115
Midland Railway 9, 11, 16, 17, 19 *seq*, 38, 82, 106, 109, 114, 132–154
Milcote 84, 85
Milkwall 50, 51
Mitcheldean 30, 38, 62, 64
    Road 62, 54
Monmouth 46, 47, 62, 65, 66–81
    May Hill 47, 69, 72, 73
    Troy 69, 72, 93
Monmouth Railway Company 47
Moreton in Marsh 93–99

Nailbridge Halt 38
Nailsworth 28, 132–138, 139
Netherhope Halt 80, 81
Newent 56, 57, 58
Newent Railway 53, 54
New Fancy junction 46
Newland 47, 48, 49
Newnham 32, 37, 38
Norchard 31, 51–52
Notgrove 104

Over junction 29, 54
Oxford, Worcester &
   Wolverhampton Railway 16, 82, 85, 97, 129

Parkend 37, 39, 42, 43, 51, 52
Park Leaze Halt 123
Pebworth Halt 85
Penallt 81

Redbrook 47, 49, 76
   Viaduct 77
Ripple 14, 15
Rodmarton Platform 123, 125
Ross & Ledbury Railway 53
Ross & Monmouth Railway
   Company 66
Ross on Wye 28, 30, 46, 59–65, 66–74
Ruspidge Halt 33, 37
Ryeford 135

St Briavels 78
Sapperton tunnel 29, 119
Serridge junction 44
Severn & Wye Joint Railway 150
Severn & Wye Railway 30 *seq*, 66 *seq*, 145, 148
Severn Bridge 144–151
Severn Valley Railway 65
Sharpness 38, 144–151
Shipston on Stour 93–99
Sling branch 50, 51
South Cerney 113
Southern Railway 114, 115
South Wales line 9, 20, 30, 38, 39, 46, 54, 59, 62, 74, 148
Speech House Road 42, 43, 44
Stanway Viaduct 83–84
Staple Edge Halt 32
Steam Mills (Crossing) Halt 36, 37, 38
Stonehouse 132 *seq*
   Bristol Road 132, 134
Stonehouse & Nailsworth Railway
   Company 132
Stow on the Wold 101, 102, 104
Stratford & Moreton Railway 93, 95

Stratford on Avon 82–92, 93, 95, 97, 98
Stretton on Fosse 97, 98
Stroud 8, 135, 136, 139–140, 144
   Wallgate 139
Swindon 104, 106–115, 118
Swindon & Cheltenham Extension
   Railway 107
Swindon, Marlborough & Andover
   Railway 106, 107
Symonds Yat 69

Tetbury 119, 123–128, 137
Tewkesbury 10 *seq*
Tewkesbury & Malvern Railway 14
Thornbury 152–154
Tidenham 81
Tintern 74, 78, 79, 81
Toddington 82, 87, 93, 94
Trouble House Halt 124, 127
Tuffley loop 21, 22, 23, 25
Tuffs junction 42
Tytherington 152, 153

Upper Soudley Halt 32

Walford Halt 70, 73
West Midland Railway 129
Weston sub Edge 85
Weston under Penyard 64
Whimsey Halt 38
Whitebrook Halt 81
Whitecliff quarry 47, 49
Whitecroft 42, 43
Willersey Halt 86
Wimberry branch 42
Winchcombe 82, 88, 89, 93, 94
Withington 109, 110
Witney 129, 130
Witney Railway 129
Woodchester 135, 137
Wyesham 47, 49, 74, 81
Wye Valley Railway 47, 74

Upton on Severn 14, 15

Yate 152, 154